WHAT PEOPLE ARE SAY

"Your words in STITCH remind me of Rodin the thinker guy, and as you know I have a place in Paris where the thinker is everywhere. And our journey as you verbalize, is who we travel with, and where we're going. As you know, I strongly believe in business, sports, and life, we need to have a map of where we're going to end, and where we're going, as it dictates, the manner in which we go. Good luck Nathan."

—Dr. Gene Landrum, founder of Chuck E. Cheese

"I have been a part of Team Nathan for a couple of years now, and I must say it has been a pleasure and an honor. He is a wizard and you don't run into many wizards these days. That he wrote a book is a gift to the rest of us. Buy it, read it, and apply it. He is the real deal. He is a creative genius and pure entrepreneur. We will see much more of him in the future. And then you can say, "I knew about him long before it was cool to do so!" Nathan has an energy that is infectious. Read his book and be inspired by his journey, his gift and his being. I love him and you will too."

—Hans Phillips, Ontoco.com

"When you look up the word entrepreneur in the dictionary a picture of Nathan Minnehan appears. Get this book and devour it. Thank me later."

—Dr. Daren Martin, The Culture Architect, A Company of Owners

"A text filled with synchronicity, dreams, and formulas to bring you everything you could ever dream of creating, tangible and intangible!"

–Allyn Reid, founder of Sherpa Press and co-creator of Secret Knock

"STITCH reminds me of the wisdom and adventure of Joseph Campbell with the great sense of mischievousness and sense of humor of Mark Twain. A must read to carry with you always."
—Craig Collins, creator of the Universal Reading Method

"STITCH is a must read for anyone looking to take a look inward, create, travel and grow."

—Frank Shankwitz, creator and a founder of the Make-A-Wish Foundation

"As unique an individual there is—that's Nathan Minnehan! And his new book, STITCH is as unique as he is because it is a collection of brilliantly crafted stories with woven wisdom throughout. Perfect reading for the expanding soul- one cool story at a time. Get started with STITCH now!"

—David M. Corbin, Mentor to Mentors, Author of Preventing Brand Slaughter, ILLUMINATE! and other groovy books.

"An amazing read."

—Dr. Greg S. Reid, Three Feet From Gold

"An entertaining and at times challenging read. Minnehan blends personal narrative with life lessons we all need to learn, and he does it seamlessly. Get this book."

—Ross Jeffries, Speed Seduction Expert and author of Subtle Words That Sell– rossjeffrieslive.com, seduction.com

"I remember the day Nate stepped foot into the room and joined my BNI chapter. Watching him grow as an entrepreneur and individual from performing a ballad he wrote for the owner of the Red Head Piano Bar when he passed, or hand-stitching 50 custom embossed wallets for all of the board members of the River North Business Association to launching his brand Big Murphy's on the 66th floor of the Sears tower at the Metropolitan club. All of it has been raw, real, and genuine. STITCH captures Nate's spirit in his entrepreneurial journey. It's the kind of book you keep with you to keep going, succeeding and seeing life as the spiritual journey it is."

—John Buckingham, Buckingham Tax and Financial, Board Member of the River North Business Association, Chicago

"I'm taking lunch, dinner, Cigar meetings all week, give me a call." Two days later Nathan and I sat together, in a quaint cigar mansion in downtown Chicago, forging an instantaneous connection equal to that of lifelong kin. Our relationship has been the catalyst for growth, change, and self reflection that most people spend a lifetime seeking; brought together by a cosmic pull that neither one of us could deny. This attraction is something I've witnessed Nathan successfully confer on countless occasions, and something which he has artfully conveyed to the readers of STITCH. Put down the testimonials, and open chapter 1."

—Dario Lobozzo, Strategic Accounts Director, SecurityMatters

"This book establishes that there is a certain kind of mindset from a certain kind of human that embodies the spirit of purpose and creativity. Our world around us is a design, a program, a system for most, but for some, it's a white canvas with every color of life available to share and inspire. Disrupting the program isn't for the faint of heart, and as entrepreneurs we tend to sail into the wind looking to fill the spinnakers energy when it's not supposed to work. As the former founder of the US pre-paid phone card industry and disruptor myself, I found this book to remind me what my direction in life is all about and Nathan, a true Renaissance man, carries a message to his audience giving them permission to sail into the wind and chase that special purpose, and live our lives, not witness them. This book is an outstanding read, and should be a reminder to all of us that we are not passengers on the ship of fools, but the captain of our own journey's. Life, it's not a practice session but a blessing beyond our wildest imaginations. Thank you, Nathan!"

—Kevin Young, a founder of the pre-paid phone card industry

"I have coached and or mentored many successful entrepreneurs over the years. The day I met Nathan in Palm Desert California, I knew there was something exceptional about this cat. It's not often I get to work with a Visionary as creative and dedicated to his craft as Nathan. Every conversation, every Tom Sawyer Tuesday, and now STITCH, leaves me with fresh and positive perspectives on whatever I'm working on at the time. Nathan's infectious energy, inspiring words and entrepreneurial spirit are without question his gift to humanity. Read and enjoy the many blessings of this gifted author. "

—Todd Thompson, Revitalization Consultant focused on Historic Business Districts, "vacant to vibrant is what we do!"

353court.com

STITCH

STITCH

THE ARTISAN ENTREPRENEUR

Nathan Minnehan

WalknTalk Books, Chicago.

STITCH
THE ARTISAN ENTREPRENEUR
By Nathan Minnehan

ISBN-13: 978-0692162194

Published by:

WALKNTALK
BOOKS

An imprint of: WalknTalk Books
1333 West Devon Ave. #226

Chicago, IL 60660-1329

TABLE OF STITCHES

PRE-STITCH

Three Keys to Success

By Dr. Greg S. Reid, autor of Three Feet From Gold

Needle and Thread
Becoming an Alchemist
Proof of Magic

Passion Stitch
Soul Stitch
About The Author

PRE-STITCH

Three Keys to Success

By Dr. Greg S. Reid, author of Three Feet From Gold

Everyone of us is born with the capacity to pursue a worthy idea, to create a brilliant life, and to build with courage. You are one of them.

I have interviewed hundreds, and maybe even thousands of people over my lifetime. From multi-millionaires to multi-billionaires. From the millionaires next door to Tonino Lamborghini, yes Mr. Lamborghini himself.

In these interviews I have found that all success boils down to one thing; perseverance. Success, like life, is an incredible process of perseverance. Did you know that when I was publishing my first New York Times Bestseller, Three Feet From Gold, I interviewed Rudy Ruettiger from the movie Rudy. Talk about perseverance. This guy was determined, not only to play football, but to tell his story.

He went out on a limb to LA to meet with a screenwriter who stood him up for lunch, then ran into a mailman outside who he told his story to, which lead to getting the screenwriter's address, and then to Rudy knocking on the guy's door to let him know he was late for lunch. The funny thing is, that screenwriter wrote his screenplay.

I opened my journal right then and wrote down: "Don't quit five minutes before the miracle happens."

The success you achieve in your life will depend on three things; the books you read, the people you meet, and the action you take.

STITCH demonstrates the type of magic that happens when you draw a line in the sand, and say "it's my turn". When you decide to live life on your terms, and call it all into question. When you decide your dreams are real, and they're yours to claim.

Just remember, most people quit right before the miracle happens. Never give up. And always be in a state of gratitude.
-Dr. Greg S. Reid

NEEDLE AND TREAD

Becoming An Alchemist

Years ago I had a dream to spread a message about personal growth through travel and student exchange. I was honored to be an exchange student after high school before college in the Czech Republic, and ever since I've felt immensely compelled to share the tools, and insights I received through this experience with dear and inspiring people I've met.

Spending my third year in college in Argentina, I began to wonder what I would pursue after finishing my degrees in Philosophy, Journalism, and Spanish Literature. I was tirelessly sewing a canvas, leather backpack in college, and made several journals as presents to bring with me for the many new friends I was destined to meet in Argentina. When I arrived, I fell in love with a woman, gifted her a journal, and then began passionately hand-staining paper with coffee on her rooftop in Buenos Aires. I was determined to creatively craft the journals I envisioned catalyzing the physicality of my message into. I believed that these journals could walk and talk, and share this message about personal growth through travel, and getting lost to find yourself.

PROOF OF MAGIC.

Over the course of a decade, my life as an entrepreneur has continued to evolve. Beginning first by inviting people to dream with my personally handcrafted leather bound journals from a yoga pillow on a purple blanket on a street corner in Buenos Aires, to then selling them from behind my leather crafted mobile bike stand on Michigan Avenue in Chicago, to then magically being featured in Time Out Chicago magazine in an article called Steal His Style, to then building my boat-like apartment and surprisingly being featured in the Chicago Reader in an article called Dreaming Big in Small Spaces, to serving pizza in a famous pizzeria in downtown Chicago to continue growing my business, to falling in love and being seduced to stay in Portugal for 45 days instead of five and missing four flights, to developing a line of my own handmade eyewear in Portugal, to hand-making over five thousand leather journals,

to working with Amish craftspeople to make the WalknTalk products, to becoming the U.S. distributor of a luxury wooden bike company from Portugal, to being spotted by best-selling author Dr. Greg Reid of Three Feet From Gold, to being featured as a speaker at his conference Secret Knock-listed as number one conference of the year by Inc Magazine in 2017, to creating a line of bespoke handmade custom suits that are now worn by leaders such as Frank Shankwitz, creator and a founder of the Make a Wish Foundation, Joerg Molt, co-founder of BitCoin, and the legendary Ross Jeffries, of Subtle Words That Sell as well as Dr. Greg Reid himself, world famous keynote speaker and author of numerous international bestselling books, not to mention other famous authors, speakers, and leaders around the world.

The journey of becoming an Artisan Entrepreneur has been one I could never trade for anything else. The shape of our lives is often determined by our abilities to find creative ways to learn, grow, and evolve. The tools that each one of these products, journeys, and mentors have given me have evolved into a set of instincts to create powerful transformation at any point in the entrepreneurial journey, and furthermore in the spiritual journey of life.

It is these tools that I have felt an overwhelming sense of urgency to share with others as to preserve their wisdom. It is furthermore an honor to personally re-introduce them to the world as they are not mine, but rather manifestations of wisdom, specs of the infinite, of the divine, God, universe.

. . .

At the heart of the meaning of the word entrepreneur in French is risk. Many wise people have said that the only risk in life is not taking a risk. Risk then arguably borders the edge of the mundane, while carefully guarding the fringe of the world of possibility.

At the core of my values has always been a desire to learn languages, and build niches around the world. To find pockets of friends who know who you are in the deepest and truest of ways.

Over the course of the past two years I decided it was time to begin communicating the drive behind my willingness to suffer countless failures, challenges, and no's along the way to creating the yes all of us long for that so often translates into our own version of true freedom. Once a week I asked a question that pertained to a particular stitch on each part of the entrepreneurial and spiritual journey of the Artisan Entrepreneur, and decided to dive in with forces of intuition, philosophy, and curiosity. I did so out of an effort to express more fully the ways we connect the dots delineating the constellations of our dreams, lives, and destinies.

No one can steal your treasure. No one can hold you back but you. No matter where you are. No matter where you're going, every stitch counts, and every moment matters. Close your eyes, breathe into your stomach, and exhale from the diaphragm, sending all doubts, fears and worries into the center of the earth. You will know what to do, and where to go.

If you're looking for a path that will lead to your life's purpose, I promise, you've found it. Sit with this book. Be with these questions, and when you feel that urge from within, follow it and don't look back. No one else needs to understand but you.
Until soon.

Yours truly,

-Nathan
#GetLostToFindYourself

STITCH

STITCH 001

Journey Into Self

"Knowledge does not come to us by details, but in flashes of light from heaven."

–Henry David Thoreau

Have you ever been on an incredible trip, feeling high on life, and then suddenly it was over? Have you ever imagined what would have happened if you stayed longer, or even dreamt of never leaving?

These are all fascinating thought experiments, and while it's not always practical to carry them out, observing and noticing them does more than one might think. It's important to take a closer look at the implications of these experiences, examining them through the lens of the WalknTalk philosophy.

The WalknTalk philosophy is a philosophy of self-creation. In order to create ourselves powerfully with intention, we must move into a space of possibility, often physically. By doing so, we are offered the opportunity to re-introduce ourselves to the world, and for the world to re-introduce itself to us.

Inside of that space of possibility we move into our most natural way of being; clear, balanced, aligned. From that place of clarity we are given access to a higher self- awareness, one that we can then integrate and weave into our lives in ways that allow us to Ground Ourselves, Propel Through Purpose, and Expand into Flow.

The Get Lost To Find Yourself initiative is key to the WalknTalk philosophy.

In December of 2014, I wrote a 'Get Lost To Find Yourself' declaration and made an event at Java's Cafe in Rochester, New York just before New Year's Eve. I had been planning to start off 2015 with a trip that would reinvent my life, and exercise the WalknTalk brand philosophy to the fullest.

THE ARTISAN ENTREPRENEUR

What followed was nothing short of extraordinary. After visiting countries in the east of Europe like Serbia, Hungary, Macedonia, and Bulgaria, I headed west to finish my "Get Lost To Find Yourself" trip with five days in Portugal – or so I thought. What followed was a moment that I call a glimpse of "re-creation."

I effectively fell in love, missed four flights, and spent forty-five days on the edge of my seat in Portugal. Besides loving every moment of it, I managed to build partnerships with wooden bike makers, a sunglasses company, even created my own line of WalknTalk boots called the Wanderers, and to top it off, met a fashion mentor that later inspired me to launch a custom suit brand called Big Murphy's.

Did I mention that I had also taken the trip with the intention of creating a video series about transforming your life with a trip?

During that time the universe placed in my path just the guys I was looking for; a whole team of videographers. Together we created this Get Lost To Find Yourself video, and many others.
www.getlostofindyourself.com

At a certain point, it becomes evident that we have exhausted our rope in making the great climb in search for meaning in all of our trips, lives, and journeys.

In that moment, we are faced with the opposite side of the circle; the third part of the journey; returning. Often returning, is a "re-turning-back towards your-self," through reintegration (coming back 'home'); integrating what you learned in order to powerfully re-create your "self" on all levels with this special knowledge. Too much too fast?

Let's begin with a simple question. What is a trip?

According to Webster's dictionary, a trip is "an act of going to a place and returning; a journey or excursion, especially for pleasure."
Now let's ask another question. What is life? ¿Qué es vida?

STITCH

In Spanish, the definition is simple: "The capacity to be born, develop, evolve, and die." Yes, even dying is part of life. Unfortunately, it is the part of life that we least appreciate and most fear. The process itself seems to be a shape though, doesn't it? Joni Mitchell called it The Circle Game:

"And the seasons they go round and round and the painted ponies go up and down. We're captive on the carousel of time. We can't return we can only look behind from where we came and go round and round and round in the circle game."

If we were to look at our 'vidas' and the trips we take as mini-lives within our life, then perhaps we wouldn't fear death so much. Perhaps we would see that in fact we are always renewing, peaking, dying, and repeating.

Journeys and Selves

Every journey has three parts: Before, during, and after, or, beginning, middle, and end. Have you ever dreamt up a trip, vacation, or a jaunt, planned it, and then worked towards it? Perhaps you bought a plane, train, or bus ticket, and then counted down the days until your trip? I bet you were excited the day before leaving and might not have even been able to sleep well the night before.

Did you ever imagine that rather than "getting away" you were actually "getting a way" into another version or possibility of you? At the core of the WalknTalk philosophy of self-creation is an idea of "getting lost to find yourself". The question becomes, which self? You might think that's a strange question. If we look at the definition of vida once again (the capacity to be born, develop, evolve, etc), wouldn't it warrant thoughts of other possible versions of ourselves being able to develop and evolve as well? After all, a "place" is a space of pure potentiality that exists as a blank canvas waiting to receive you. Almost like soil waiting for seeds.

Before we can go further, we must ask: what is leaving?

Webster dictionary defines leaving as "to allow to remain, or to go away from." Does that not imply that a part of us stays? And what was it again that life does? Evolve, develop, die? Unless otherwise preserved, one might say?

THE ARTISAN ENTREPRENEUR

Imagine yourself again at the end of an incredible trip. You're on cloud nine. New people have entered into your life. You have entered into other people's lives. The version of you the night before your trip even began compared with who you are now is somehow different. Something has shifted. The unknown trip has now revealed itself.

But what about the third part of the trip, the leaving, the letting go, and even the forgetting?

Is it really possible that you somehow remain "existing" in another place, or for that place to remain "existing" in you? Well, ask yourself this question: are you not many things? Thoughts, ideas, sounds, expressions, gestures, feelings... Are they not parts of you? Are these parts not transferable? Must you remain for them to remain as well?

"No man ever steps in the same river twice, for it's not the same river and he's not the same man" – Heraclitus.

This Greek proverb points to this subtlety. It also says that experience is real, tangible, and alive. As we affect the world around us, so we are also affected. Is this not where we form lenses to craft our vision and become Visionaries? www. visionaryframes.club

Lenses? Yes, an experience can be seen as a metaphor for a lens that we use to craft our vision.

As you can see we have ventured into some pretty abstract territory here, and you're probably wondering where this is all going. Well, that's how I usually felt reading philosophy texts in college. I confess I always wished there were videos that could facilitate my contemplation, something that could bring the text to life. Well, they say that yearning leads to creating. My hope is for this text to be a river carrying inspiration, and creative thoughts, things, and ideas to you. Watch the video in the link above (www.visionaryframes.club).

STITCH 002

Magical Powers

"Ground Yourself. Propel through Purpose. Expand into Flow."

-WalknTalk Manifesto

Have you ever felt like you had magical powers? Like you were capable of doing anything you set your mind to? I mean, if someone asked you, "are you powerful," how would you respond?

Would it depend on when they asked you, how you were feeling that day, or how much confidence you had in that moment? Where would you look for evidence to make that response, and stake your claim? I hope your response is an immediate "yes," but what if it isn't?

Is there a clause? Is there some kind of syllogism you need to use to prove that you have magical powers, use them, and are powerful? Is your entire equation only valid when a certain variable is not in play? Is there a certain place or person in your life that can take away your magical powers? Is it painful or scary to even consider these questions? Good. That means there is something useful waiting on the other side.

The other side? Yes. We will be taking a walk through time, crossing rivers, and imagining what our lives would look like if only we had time to see them. See them? Yes, see them. (Hint, hint)

"All consciousness is consciousness of something."-Immanuel Kant

Becoming aware of where we are placing our consciousness, might be the first step into building a better ability to live life powerfully. An elderly Sri Lankan Buddhism professor named Dr. Wicks once told me, "my friend, the only path worth taking is the path leading in." He then said, "the only thing worth doing is teaching."

THE ARTISAN ENTREPRENEUR

But must we not "do" first in order to teach later? And what happens if we are too "busy" or too "scared" to "do," and then miss out on the teaching?" Could the sensation of "jumping with courage" (traveling with purpose) be the one antidote to fear, meltdown, and everything else that truly gets in the way of living empowered lives?

Why don't we take this opportunity to pull the magnifying glasses from our backpacks, hold them up to the moments in our lives when we can notice these subtle shifts happening, and simply and humbly say "that's interesting." Without these shifts we wouldn't be human. So rather than finding fault here, let's keep being the philosopher, and receive the diamond cut key on the other side of this process.

Many kids grow up feeling oppressed. Whether it's because of schoolwork, friends, or family trouble, we all know emotions can run high. It's usually as a result of these emotions that we choose a particular direction in our lives. But when do we get permission to stop running in that direction, drop the anger, fear, doubt, or pity, and just say "okay. It's okay; I'm okay. Now what?" What such moment would be unique enough to create such a new direction, and what would that make possible?

How about a trip, a new beginning? According to our WalknTalk philosophy, every journey has three parts: Before, during, and after. Almost like your life, a trip can be a new beginning, and a vehicle for personal growth and transformation. It starts with wanting to live a change, then going and living it, and lastly integrating it back into our lives. Being the transformed you, powerfully. As a teenager I struggled with a mixture of those ingredients stated above. I imagined what it would be like to learn a new language, make new friends, and open a new chapter in my life. Becoming an exchange student made that possible. Not only did it open a new chapter in my life, but it opened a new chapter in me, almost as if I grew up a second time. The place I went to became a new home, and it seemed as though everything there was possible: finding a community of friends, living good life, becoming an artist, and most specifically, creating myself on purpose. Over the years, the third part of these trips has been the most challenging; the end, "going home." This is when the "shift" usually always happened.

Why? Because of something called: Old Self versus New Self.

STITCH

Growing means changing. When we return from transformative trips, that change is not always known or honored by others.

Each one of the trips we take shows us a new facet of who we are, and who we are becoming. They are glimpses into our desired realities; distant dreams not so distant. They give us knowledge about how to create that transformation in our own lives, and then present the opportunity to do so upon returning "home". If you think about it, flying high in the sky, or traveling miles by car or train, leads to thinking. This is when many of us do our best journaling, including myself. What if we began to see trips as vehicles for forming ourselves into who we truly wish to become? Like mini retreats custom built for our own specific needs and desires.

Is there anything wrong with wanting to be someone else? Well, I'm not sure if it's really about wanting to be someone else, but rather about wanting to express and become what is begging to be explored. Something that is somehow otherwise denied expression because of where we are physically and/ or emotionally. I believe there is something inside of all of us that wishes to be created, expanded, and transformed. The word courage comes from the Latin word "cor" which means heart (Corazon;Spanish, Cuore;Italian). It indeed takes courage to take a journey to another part of the world or country. Especially, when it involves extended stays, building niches in new cultures, and learning a new language. What it also requires is faith, faith that something incredible is in progress.

These ingredients often lead to stories that can be put in books, and made into movies. It is no wonder why revisiting these journeys gives us courage, and faith that we can once again take on whatever else comes our way.

When we find ourselves forgetting about who we are, or noticing a voice in our head that has shifted us, we can be sure that we have left our hearts. Often I'll notice when this is happening, and be lucky enough to meet someone new, and reintroduce myself. The reintroducing causes me to remember the real me, the truest and most powerful self. But what do you mean? I mean that telling my story, stating my purpose, and what I am up to in building my vision, is what brings the focus back to my core, placing my focus back in my heart. If we think about what happens when we shift from living our lives in our head to living it in our hearts, we notice something else that is going on. We are connected to our story, our purpose, and our vision. A few years ago I was sitting on my graphic designer's back deck working on the WalknTalk manifesto poster called "Get Lost To Find Yourself." The following phrases came to me. It is in these phrases that we can find that diamond cut key, and use it to unlock our desired realities and become the stealth, staunch, healthy versions of ourselves at any given moment.

"Ground Yourself, Propel through Purpose, Expand into Flow" These phrases became the WalknTalk Manifesto.

STITCH 003

Being The Magic

"Oh me! Oh Life!"

-Whitman

Have you ever felt like you are so overwhelmed by the details that you forget to take a breath and realize the main focus? Have you ever taken a moment to consider why dialogue has the power to take us beyond the here and now, and visit places of understanding within ourselves that somehow unlock the next step in this incredible journey of awakening?

There is one key powerful component to this journey that continues to baffle me every time I realize it.

That is the power of "the story." That's right. The story, the myth, the legend, that is our life, has more power locked inside of it than in the entire 110 floors of the Sears Tower. The process of awakening to our potential is just that: a process, one of remembering, connecting the dots, and conducting the symphony. To put it simply, 'being with the magic'.

"Magic is in the stories we tell, and the intention we live with"

-The Wizard Oz

Sitting perched in my workshop, with the window open and the sound of birds chirping streaming in from over the treetops, my mind moved from one subject to the next as I gathered the strength to manage a deluge of possibility. When faced with many tasks, I open to a clean sheet in my journal, and map out the bigger picture. I compare the bigger picture to the smaller picture of my immediate to-do list and then dive in.

Like many, "diving in" is often a process of summoning focus and gathering inspiration.

THE ARTISAN ENTREPRENEUR

In doing so, I stumbled across this quote in a short film. It occurred to me that so much of the joy experienced in life evolves from moments of sharing stories, and recalling our great feats. As if we must go, have adventures daily, and then only when coming together to share our experiences, can we tighten the web and truly see the interconnectedness of our journeys.

It was said that Mark Twain would work all day only to stand up and entertain his family with tales of Tom Sawyer and the like by night.

Could it be that reading what he wrote gave him the insight and courage to write the next chapter? What if he was discouraged? Do you think Mark Twain would be discouraged?

Of course he could be. He was human.

However, the difference between Twain succeeding and failing was a decision to keep on "singing."

In high school I had a teacher that would famously say, "boys, sing yourselves!" -Mrs. Bors.

Mimicking scenes from the Dead Poets Society, she would demand we stand on our chairs and "sing the song of ourselves."
"From the diaphragm," she would insist.

"Sound your barbaric YAWP over the rooftops of the world!" She would say, in the words of Whitman.

Ruminating on these thoughts I boarded a train heading to downtown for an event. Sitting on the train I received a phone call from a special friend. Not wanting to disturb others, and desiring to fully engage the conversation, I stepped off onto the platform. We talked for a while until it dawned on me that being on time and speaking in quiet would require calling an UBER.

Getting into the front seat, I looked behind me only to notice two beautiful people.

STITCH

"Craig you wouldn't believe it, but there are two beautiful people in the back seat of this UBER."

Laughing like a Jack-o-Lantern, I maintained my awkward position with my head twisted around talking with them.

"You'll never believe who I'm talking to," I said. "I met this person on a train to New York five years ago, and I swear to you, it changed my life forever. We've stayed in touch over Skype, Facebook, and the phone. He has introduced me to this incredible group of entrepreneurs in California where I'm actually going next week!"

They seemed a bit confused, but wound up excited to hear more. I continued.

"The inventor of the magnetic strip on credit cards, velcro, UGG Boots, and all sorts of other people are going to be there. I'm donating one of our wooden bikes from Portugal, and somehow getting a chance to talk on stage; it's going to be great! Can you believe it?"

The two people laughed.

"What do you do?" I asked.

"I work for a non-profit, and we're actually throwing a big event in June," one said.

"That's great, have you ever thought about joining other networking groups to grow your non-profit?" I said. I told them about the Metropolitan Club and what a great spot it is to meet people. Their stop came, and eventually we parted ways. I continued my conversation with my friend on the phone.

Speaking into my phone, I said, "See? Magic. Whenever we get together, it's just great. When you engage the moment in story and open yourself up to the world, anything is possible!"

Craig chuckled on the other side of the line.

"So, when are you coming to California?" he asked. "Tuesday," I said.

THE ARTISAN ENTREPRENEUR

"No, when are you moving to California?" He said. I laughed.

"We'll see," I said.

Later, at a Toastmasters speaking event, I sat in a quiet room in the Westin on Dearborn and Kinzie. A hush came over the group. The speaker was in transition in the front of the room as the next Toastmaster took the stage.

The night went on, and before departing we enjoyed cocktails in the lobby that smelled like white tea air fresheners.

A trickling fountain ran in the corner, as I looked around scouting for a seat. Sitting down next to the "new guy," I turned to him and introduced myself.

"Hey I'm Nathan, what's your name?"

"Joe," he said.

"Where ya from Joe?" I said.

"Just moved from Philly, originally from Brasil."

"A serio?" I said in Portuguese.

"Claro." He said.

"Que bom," I replied.

An incredible conversation ensued in Portuguese for about an hour in which I told him of my incredible adventures in Portugal, and how I got started making leather goods, eyewear, journals, bags, and the like. As I told him the story in my good but growing level of fluency, he paid close attention.

"So you met some guys in Portugal that make videos, glasses, and wooden bikes? And you stayed there for forty-five days?" he clarified.

"Yes," I answered, still speaking in Portuguese. "I met a Native American in Seattle years ago who was carving canoes by hand with children at a place called the Center

STITCH

for Wooden Boats. He took me for a ride on his hand carved canoe one day, and whispered a phrase to me that I have lived by ever since." I paused. "Be Strong, and Follow the Spirit."

"Que bom," He smiled, shaking his head and grinning.

"Say, I'd love to show you around the city, let's keep in touch, and get something on the books soon," I said.

With that, we exchanged information and planned to keep in touch. I couldn't help but feel like I understood more about life by telling my story again. By just being open, and sharing the journey I've been on with the world.

Two days later, back in Chicago, I met the people from the UBER in the Metropolitan Club in the Sears Tower for lunch.

"The lady of the hour, a tower of power, too sweet to be sour!" I said, repeating an old phrase from my golf coach in New York.

We chuckled and grabbed a table to have lunch. It was a woman and her brother. They were both on a mission to connect more people to beauty and meaning in life with their non-profit. They loved the idea of doing so with custom journals and enjoyed the view as we spoke for what felt like hours.

In their departure, I grabbed a stool by the window overlooking the tremendous cityscape from the 67th floor.

I thought of Whitman. I thought of my teacher from Poetry class. I thought of my dear friend from the train. Crossing my legs, while shaking my head, nodding and smiling I thought:
Story... Palabra... 'strangers'... family... connection...

My mind drifted back to that poetry class in High School and to a poem from the Dead Poets Society.

"Oh me! Oh Life! Of the questions of the recurring; of the endless trains of the faithless... of the cities filled with the hopeless. What good amid these?"

THE ARTISAN ENTREPRENEUR

Answer:

"That we are here, and that life exists, and identity; that the powerful play goes on and that we may contribute a verse. That the powerful play goes on, and you may contribute a verse. What will your verse be?" –Whitman

"Sound your barbaric YAWP over the rooftops of the world!" -Whitman

"YAWP!"

(Want to see my YAWP in 2012? Watch this video until the end: (www.walkntalk. us)

STITCH 004

On the Right Track

"If the doors of perception were cleansed, everything would appear as it is, infinite."

–Aldous Huxley

Have you ever wondered what that feeling is that urges us to take action, but is so often disrupted by fear and anxiety? Have you ever considered mastering it? Or even wondered what could be possible if we did?

I would like to tell you a story about how talking with a stranger on a train three years ago led to an opportunity to consult with Billionaires poolside in Palm Springs, about how to grow my business, and hopefully bring the WalknTalk message worldwide. While the "B" word may have your head spinning (as it did mine), let's not lose track of the deeply meaningful message contained within this true tale that begs to be examined.

It all started one dark ominous night at Union Station in Chicago. I was holding two one hundred pound suitcases full of leather journals—that's right, one hundred pounds each – my guitar, and my hand-stitched backpack that took me three years to make in college.

If you've ever boarded a train in Union Station you'd recall the soot and sound of the gritty tracks that reek of a period in time that most of us do not remember. I felt like a modern Woody Guthrie ready to climb up into a boxcar. When in reality I was an artisan heading to his first out of state fair with way too much merchandise. It was there alongside me that stood a smiling face with a straw hat. He said "You seem like an interesting person. I'd love to know your life story. If you'd like, I'll be sitting up in the front, and you're welcome to join me."

THE ARTISAN ENTREPRENEUR

"That's a bit forward," I thought. On one hand, I did want to talk with him, but my better judgment told me to wait until the morning.

Morning came and the white noise of clanking carts and passing country pasture was nicely accented by the voices of a few Amish folks sitting in the booth across the aisle. I naturally greeted them and told them of my working relationship with the Amish in the Midwest. It was then that I looked over, and noticed not all the straw hats were Amish. Nestled in the booth behind them was that same smiling face from the night before.

"Hi I'm Craig. It's so nice to meet you," he said.

In an instant we began a conversation that barely had enough brakes to stop at my station, and quite honestly had enough speed that it could have continued straight into the heart of the Atlantic Ocean.

We spoke on Skype later that night, and on into the future. He became a friend and resource that I could truly count on. Someone that understood the mad, mystical journey that so definitely defined my life.

Every once in a while, we meet someone that willingly shares the keys to doors leading to life's windows of opportunity. Those doors were opened via Facebook when Craig decided there were people who I "needed" to meet. I added about thirty or more of these folks on Facebook, one of which was a keynote speaker. I've always aspired to write books and become a speaker, so naturally I was intrigued.

Three years passed, and this keynote speaker kept popping up in my Facebook newsfeed. I'd notice interesting self-made memes that he would post. One of which said "If you're in my rear view, and would like to be in my inner circle, message me."

I finally decided: why not? It was in that moment that a west coast number showed up on my phone. I picked up and the window of opportunity opened. He was very brief, congratulating me on building a neat company, and made me an offer to come out west for a special conference. I couldn't possibly reject the offer, so I said "yes," a word that always leads to adventure, and engages possibility.

STITCH

A second window opened when he offered up another opportunity. I said yes again, and decided I would figure out a way. When I hung up the phone, I felt as if I had just been soaked by a giant wave of opportunity. One that somehow came steaming from the Pacific Ocean via the light in that smiling man's eyes from the train. When I was a kid my father talked about Chicago being the gateway to the west. When people would ask why I live there alone, I'd usually tell them, "it's the gateway city".

I realize that there are gates everywhere in our lives. Rather than wonder about the ones we've missed, why not ask "what would it take to be present to our ability to say yes when fear tells us to say no?" After all, fear seems to be opportunity's greatest disguise, and the only thing standing between us and our freedom to "live, write, now."

Hint: Lean into possibility with your pen over a journal, and dare to write what you dream to live now. Then find the patience, courage, and audacity to let now be anytime, anywhere.

STITCH 005

Follow the Spirit

"The two most important days in your life are the day you were born, and the day you find out why."

– Mark Twain

Have you ever wondered how it's possible that the universe is able to engineer such moments of sheer wisdom through the most uncanny and marvelous scenarios that truly make real life "even better than fiction"?

Years ago as an exchange student in Prague, Czech Republic, 2007, I made friends with a kid named David whose dad used to bring him Jack Kerouac books from his trips to the United States. The two of us bonded through our love of the novel On the Road, and had a dream to do a road trip around the country. A year later I returned to Prague for a visit, and he and I and another Czech pal, Adam, were sitting in a Czech Café called 67. Adam and I were both artisans and really bonded through our individual approaches to hand making leather products.

Crafts aside, we were all determined to make a trip happen during the upcoming summer, and vowed to see it through.

When they finally arrived we bought a truck for one hundred dollars, put a cap on the back, sealed it with liquid nails, and made it our caravan for a brilliant thirty five day, seventy five hundred mile trek around the USA. Yes the truck needed work, but somehow we nursed it through the trip over blistering hot highways, and up steep mountain passes.
On our trip, it became apparent that we would all need a break from each other, and from the bench seat we somehow managed to ride on for three thousand miles to the West Coast. It seems that the alone time we needed came at the perfect moment, as we had just pulled into Seattle, and I was inspired to check out a wooden boat center I had heard about.

THE ARTISAN ENTREPRENEUR

Walking up to a sign that said "Center for Wooden Boats," I had a feeling I was in the right place. To my right was a man standing there with his daughter. To my left was a tree trunk laying under an open-air pavilion that appeared to be carved down the middle. I soon found out that it was a handmade canoe in progress, and that the Native American carving it was doing so with children on the weekends. I told the man and his daughter how much I loved wooden boats, and how I'd worked on a 100-year-old wooden sailboat as a teenager with my godfather. We walked around the docks examining the marvelous collection of skiffs. The man said it was a shame that the carver was not there that day as he was a very wise man, and known to speak in simple ways that left lasting impressions. I sat down on a bench on the dock, and began eating a sandwich. I was journaling about this incredible place I had stumbled upon, and regretted having to leave so soon. After a long moment, I began packing up to reunite with my Czech pals to continue our journey down the West Coast.

As I turned the corner to leave, I noticed a man of unmistakable stature winding up a hose on the dock. He was dressed in denim from head to toe, and wore a black pony- tail with shaved sides above his ears. I wandered up to him and said: "Hey are you Sazzuuts?"

"I am Sáádúúts, and who are you?" He replied. "My name is Nathan." I said innocently.

"My son's name is Nathan..." His voice was deep, slow, and powerful. I began telling him about the boatyard that I grew up working in, and the old wooden sailboat that taught me so much about life. I told him how much I admired the canoes he had carved. There were two finished ones tied up to the dock mooring directly beside us.

"Do you want to go for a ride?" He said rather seriously.

I couldn't believe my ears. I'm pretty sure I even squealed as I said "yes," still working my way through disbelief. He stared straight through my eyes, and then pointed to a barrel of wooden paddles directly behind me.

"Grab two paddles, " he said. I slowly stepped back, and latched onto the first one. It was as light as a feather, and hand-carved from yellow cedar.

STITCH

What happened in the next hour was perhaps the most remarkable moment in my life. It marked a fundamental before and after, and left me muttering a phrase that is still open for interpretation. We stepped into the canoe. It was like nothing I had ever touched: Cold, heavy, sturdy, and charged with the feeling of the wilderness. As we embarked, he pulled a McDonald's cup from the water, and said, "She's very sick brother... We have to take care of her." (Referring to mother nature). We passed under a bridge, and made our way out into the lake. I sat perched on the front of the canoe. Pebbles of sound dribbled into the water... The voice from behind me called and said.

"Nathan," there was a pause. "Just enjoy your life, brother. Be Strong and Follow the Spirit..."

A shiver of Goosebumps ran up my spine. What I was questioning about life, during a period of spiritual inquisition was suddenly solved. In an instant, any doubts I had harbored were suddenly vanquished. And with the stillness of the moment, the pendulum in my chest was positively reset. I am forever grateful for that day, that moment, and that gift.

In the past ten years of travel I have been noticing a pattern, there is something very peculiar that happens on these kinds of adventures that I've been talking about. It seems to happen spontaneously, but only after certain steps are taken.

What are the steps? Great Question. It's simple.

Expand. Intuit. Flow. Or in other words: plan a trip to expand who you are, set an intention, and then have the courage to follow the flow of events without expectation. Is it really that simple? Are you just playing us based on your cool experience with Sáádúúts? Ha! Wish I could tell you that I was, but no, I'm serious about this.

There is one important thing to recall though. Transforming through trips often requires taking risks, spending money, time, and energy all in the effort of no regrets. If you're up for that sort of task, then you should ask yourself when you're planning to take your next I.V. (Inspiration Vacation). After all, we can't exactly rewind the tape of life. We have to find the courage to tear the moment open, and make space for grace to piece it back together. It's often in those moments of strong resistance that a new layer of life is waiting to be revealed.

STITCH 006

Inspiration Vacation

"We must be willing to get rid of the life we've planned so as to have the life that is waiting for us."

–Joseph Campbell, The Hero's Journey

Have you ever heard people speak about following your bliss? Or seen YouTube videos of eloquent contrarians telling you why to not follow your bliss? Or even wondered what your bliss truly is?

It doesn't take a rocket scientist to know when someone you meet has discovered "it" while others you encounter maybe have not.

The truth is we are all born into a current; a flow of energy created by systems put into place long before we've arrived. These systems include, family, government, 'education', language, and more. By default we are mandated to conform to a culture, and if and when we resist, we are shunned. However, beyond judgments of good or bad regarding these systems, is a much more valuable subject, that when learned and leveraged, can open up a world far greater than one could ever have imagined.

"Give me a lever long enough, and a fulcrum on which to place it, and I shall move the world." –Archimedes

The American Literature Professor and author Joseph Campbell, wrote about something called the Hero's Journey. His life's work surrounded the topic of "Following your bliss" talking about how "the universe will open doors for you where there were only walls."

To some who have never experienced this, the idea sounds like a sham, but to others who have, the phrase makes perfect sense.

Why? What begins as a small hint of curiosity often leads to a magnetic pursuit into an entirely unique parallel universe, and world of magical possibilities.

THE ARTISAN ENTREPRENEUR

Many of us search for these possibilities in things, when in fact they can only be created through experiences. One such way I have discovered into this transformation of discovering one's bliss is through learning languages, and recreating ourselves as we've always wished to be; fully self-actualized, aware, dream-realizing, and energetically high on life, people.

It is no secret that to spend time in different places, surrounded by different cultures, somehow begins a process of transforming the mindset of an individual.

In the United States, an affluent first world country, it is still seen as unique to speak more than one language, while in Europe it is commonplace to speak several. Given what we all observe about others that travel and learn languages there is something that happens to them while going through the experience that makes us all yearn for it as well.

In a secular sense they are reborn. With a new language comes a new identity. In a world where Amazon Prime can bring you just about anything in 24 hours or less, identity is sexy, mysterious, and this kind, not for sale.

The identity one finds, and creates brings with it a unique set of possibilities. Like a seed stuck into soil, ideas from other cultures when planted into a foreign person create in them a hybrid way of being.

According to contemporary life coaches applying Ontology, the study of being originally uncovered by 20th century philosophers like Husserl in the realm of Phenomenology, there is a consensus among them that certain "ways of being" either grant you access to possibility or not.

According to Accomplishment Coaching, and the original engineer of this idea for the company, Hans Phillips of Ontoco, when an individual is in his or her "essence," he or she naturally receives life's wonderful possibilities as opposed to when he or she is not "being" in his or her essence, in which case "possibilities" are not naturally available to that person.

This begs the question...

STITCH

How often are individuals not in their "essence," but rather caught in someone else's web? And what limitations could such a scenario put on one's ability to build a brilliantly inspired life on purpose while in such circumstances? Studies show that a large percentage of Americans have less than two thousand dollars in savings, an average of $200,000 in student loan debt, carry a balance on credit cards, and are often paying car notes they truly cannot afford.

It is easy to see how one could become swept up into a system that acts like a conveyor belt ushering along others to follow suit even though it obviously does not make sense to do so.

You might wonder why as a culture so many people would continue down a path that sounds so uninspired, and in fact not much fun at all?

I am not your guru, but here is my two cents.
The blind are leading the blind. Too often, youth look to elders who grew up in a world that no longer exists, and take advice that no longer applies, i.e. go to college, get a job, get married, have kids, be a good citizen. While there is nothing wrong with this, there are other formulas that DO work, and can create extraordinary results.

When given a finite number of subjects to study, and professions to take on, people often lose sight of the possibility of creating their own profession / streams of income independent of the options laid out on a college class sheet.

In the past five years I have spent 6 weeks to 12 weeks at a time in three of the five years in different countries during my annual inspiration vacation (IV), and the other two in the U.S. in increments of 3,6, and 10 week IV's manifesting incredible experiences of love, and building out the businesses that I was originally inspired to create during those first three years of extended time spent abroad.

How? I decided I would create a path that would allow me to create flexible income, and the freedom to take long breaks for continued growth and personal development such as: learning languages, making friends in other countries, building relationships with factories and international entrepreneurs to leverage multiple income streams, and take advantage of time well spent investing in myself in an effort to "Ground myself, Propel through purpose, and expand into flow," –the WalknTalk Manifesto.

THE ARTISAN ENTREPRENEUR

(What if you only have ten days? Start with ten, and be open to receiving the unique offer the universe will most certainly make you. Follow the next clue into creating your life on purpose, free, and limitless.)

When living our everyday lives, we cannot help but become subject to the inundation of events that so often pull us out of our essence, ostracizing us from possibility, and our highest truly expressed versions of ourselves.

In order to encounter bliss we must take a moment to minimize the noise of life. In the language of Husserl, the phenomenologist who originally studied the essence of things, we must "bracket our existence" and move into a new space of possibility.

An inspiration vacation is a trip designed to bracket your mundane life for the extended period of time to afford you the ability to move into a parallel reality; a world of possibilities unencumbered by the stress of infinite to-do's and constructions shaping you that are limitations that have been set by a society's flow of energy that is simply one possible way of being among thousands of other possible constructions of life on earth.

An IV is meant to be an IV for the real you, a ripcord that you pull to stop the free- fall, and zap you back into a place of power, health, and wellbeing with massive perspective to guide you to make empowered life decisions as you move forward.

When you move into a space that is "other," possible, and uniquely set up to evolve what is at the forefront of what you've always wished you had time to do, you are literally stepping into a place the universe has reserved for you, or in the words of Joseph Campbell "the life that is waiting for us".

The energy of the space you create during your inspiration vacation is light, adventurous, and infinite. The idea of anything is possible, is the energy that you will find in this other space.

If you are someone who can never get a date…

If you are someone who has no idea what they want to do… If you are wondering what is next in your life…

STITCH

If you are longing for life to make sense…

All of these are indicators that you are looking at life through a lens that needs a new prescription.

Consider letting an inspiration vacation re-craft your vision, and give you a perspective you've been yearning for all along.

Inspiration Vacation Continued…

Despite the beautiful claims of Joseph Campbell that we "must be willing to get rid of the life we've planned so as to have the life that is waiting for us," many people simply do not know how to do this, or feel they are too scared to try.

It is helpful to know that Campbell is most famous for also saying "the cave we fear to enter holds the treasure we seek."

Looking for an example of an I.V.?

In January of 2015, I set out on what was to be a six-week journey around Europe, my usual winter trip. However, this year I was set on creating a video series called Inspiration Vacation: transform your life with a trip. In the midst of making the video and the travel, I actually lived the experience I had been dying to report on. I ended up falling in love in Portugal, missing four flights, and staying there for forty-five days instead of five, the original plan. Yes, sometimes life is messy, but in that mess is tremendous possibility.

"Embrace the sacred messiness of life." Rabbi Irwin Kula, Yearnings

During my time in Portugal I literally moved through one experience after the other discovering mentors, and finding clues that would lead me to believe that my life today would not be complete without this experience. In just one trip, love found a way to distract me long enough to see a bigger possibility, life in Portugal. While I was aware enough to resist the temptation to play it safe, and return on time, I took a lot financial risk by staying. When put into perspective the financial risk was literally nothing years later as it afforded me tools that I could not live my current life without.

THE ARTISAN ENTREPRENEUR

The friends that came into my life from that trip literally invigorated my life on every level: business, personal, physical, lingual, gastronomic, geographic, etc.
In those 45 days I literally formed such a powerful association with Portugal that it has gone on to be the secret blessing that life had been waiting to give me.

While there is not necessarily one "bliss" that I discovered there, but rather a multitude, there is on the other hand a few clues pointing toward a formula for discovering one's bliss.

Take for instance the resistance we all feel toward the "how" we are going to make a certain trip happen.

Imagine that resistance is actually a locked treasure box that only appears in the back of one's mind when one is reminded of a dream one has.

Take for instance the dream of going to Europe if you have not been before, or another continent you dream of travelling to.

In comparison to the life you are living in your current place, that distant dream seems steeped in possibility, and ripe for the most incredible experiences life could offer.

When you imagine going there, your mind moves into a space of possibility.

Then the dog barks, and you return to the mundane, realizing you have chores to do, and errands to run.

When we set the intention to move confidently with purpose into that dream in the form of taking a trip we begin peeling back that fine line between possible and impossible, mundane and out of this world.
As we move into possible, and out of the mundane we also leave a space of infinite to-do's and undone tasks behind to receive an infinite world of possibilities waiting to greet us in the place we imagine going to.

As we bring the fleeting dream front and center, and begin acting on its behalf, making it real, instead of avoiding it, we begin trusting intuitively, not in something we can definitely be sure of, but in something we can no longer live without discovering for ourselves.

It is in this space of trusting that we are given a pathway into a world primed for bliss that once discovered becomes so undeniable that we are in fact as Campbell says nearly "willing to get rid of the life we've planned (or the one we are taking a break from by being on this trip) so as to have the life that is waiting for us."

Of course not everyone is going to stay in Europe, China, South America, or wherever they have dreamt of going to. However, the possibilities made visible to them through the experience have not only transformed their self awareness, but given them the ability now know more intuitively how valuable the journey is for them, and for others making it.

Therefore, what I have come to understand is that a trip is a vehicle. Whatever you're looking to evolve in your life can be done at fantastical speeds when you bring your vision with you into a space of possibility; into the unknown.

IV Equation (www.inspirationvacation.org)

+Belief in possibility and in yourself

+ The courage to go to a new place (preferably foreign and preferably alone as not to bring any remnants of the mundane or the 'you' that others have limited you as, including your partner—this is not meant as a 'negative' limitation but rather in the sense of the partner being someone you already know, limits the neutrality of the world around you to re-introduce itself to you).

+ You re-introducing yourself, and your dreams to the world and people seeing you in your inspired essence, being yourself outside of your mundane existence.

+ An open mind to be honest with yourself and who you wish to become through that experience.

+ The magic of the trip and the universe conspiring in your favor.

THE ARTISAN ENTREPRENEUR

= You high on life and your intention for your trip blossoming tenfold before your eyes.

What else is possible with your IV?

STITCH 007

I Heard God Laughing

"Cast all your votes for dancing."

–Hafiz

I'd like to tell you a story about how a mini family Inspiration Vacation salted with intention has led to an abundance of laughter, creativity, and contemplation.

Often to fully appreciate the moments we create, and the instincts with which we create them, we must look at the moments of learning from which they arise. Perhaps these are moments from our past, from places far away. For me, they are from people in those places, and one in particular I must reference in full detail to grant the proper perspective to view these events.

"Every phenomenon appears, but it appears only to the extent that it shows itself."

–Jean Luc Marion

Years ago I met a gaucho on a ranch in Argentina who told me a story about how he once hitchhiked to Antarctica with a book that changed his life forever. The book was called I Heard God Laughing and was written by a 14th century poet named Hafiz.

The day I met him I had travelled via omnibus with my study abroad group in Argentina, from Buenos Aires to the small but legendary town of San Antonio de Areco.
There in the town square I sat playing my guitar, blowing on my harmonica, and singing songs like 'blowing in the wind' by Bob Dylan.

A man dressed in pants tapered at the bottom, a beret, and wearing a beard like mine walked up and said hello.

THE ARTISAN ENTREPRENEUR

He said to me, "My friend, learn to recognize the counterfeit coins that will buy you one moment of pleasure, but then drag you for days like a broken man behind a farting camel." -Hafiz

He didn't mean to be so direct, but poetry to him, I soon learned, was like air, and he breathed it everywhere he went.

He told me about his travels to the United States, and his time in Hollywood, studying in acting school for free with some of the world's most famous actors. Of course, like me at the Prague film school, he had found his way for free into the acting college by being of service, and no one really asked why he was there.

During his announcements later on to the group at the ranch, I learned that he spoke Spanish, Italian, and French as well. I also learned he was sincere, and in the moments of my departure, walking across the pampas, I learned he was bold.

I heard my name blasting through a megaphone.

"Nathan, keep it real brother!"

I checked my email two days later and found this...

HERE WE MEET AT THE TEMPLE'S GATES. I CELEBRATE THE JOY OF ENCOUNTERING THIS... "U" SHAPE OF OUR SAME SOUL.
WE ARE THE RIVER, ITS CREATURES, AND THE VERY FLOW... WITHIN THE SEED, THERE ARE THE BRANCHES OF THE TREE, AND THE FRUITS, AND THE SHADE. BE MERRILY YOU, IN GLADNESS AND CONFIDENCE. WE ARE INSTRUMENTS...WHAT GUILDED KARMA HERMANO!

I respond:

The garden enjoys a blossoming bloom because butterfly wings flutter subtle sweet truths to the messengers at the gate. The gorge echoes songs of running rivers throughout the treacherous forests. Two men take heed to the voice of the heartless and turn to take up a forged arm of parallel post.

STITCH

Unspoken words sail, singing soulfully on swells in the cloudy blue sky, one by the other they go on…strumming…DANCING to the minstrel tune and its everlasting twine!

A cornucopia of blessings to you Juan Manuel!!

He responds:

SERENDIPITY.
JOY.
BLESSINGS TAKING FLIGHT ALL ABOUT US.
FLATTERBYS.
LONGINGS AND CERTANTIES. GOD IS AT HAND.
A ZILLION PARTICLES LINGER IN
UNCOMPREHENSIBLE HARMONY.
AIR TICKLES.
SPIRITUAL HONEYMOONERS.
THANKSGIVING.

Nine months later I traveled back to San Antonio de Areco with my girlfriend, and a close friend of ours. I walked into the room where Juan Manuel had been announcing months before. It felt empty in the space though there were many people seated in the front of the room.

I walked over next to him, and rested an elbow at the bar in the back where he was standing. I stared at him saying nothing at all. And then in a moment of great ecstasy he realized who I was, and we were reunited at last.

THE ARTISAN ENTREPRENEUR

That evening we sat in the coziness of a home he had built with his bare hands for his mother. He invited us to drink wine, and coffee. Our friend played the piano while my girlfriend and I sat on the couch. The house was filled with pictures of him with famous actors, and the spirit of a very worldly, cultured man despite the very rural location where he was residing.

I wondered what kept him there in that small town, and recalled the book he had spoke of. Had I known the book the Alchemist at the time I would have thought he was an alchemist.

The night moved on with passion as the piano seemed to soften subtle moments of awkward discomfort between us.

And in one moment of curiosity I asked about an interesting pillow on the couch. It was in that moment he informed us all that it was in fact a pillowcase housing a sleeping bag. It happened to be the same sleeping bag he used to hitch hike to Antarctica, and the same one that kept him warm as he soaked in the wisdom of the text he nine months earlier had revealed to me in such eloquent prose.

Lying there on his fireplace hearth was the original copy of the book tattered from his journey he so nostalgically recanted to us. Including the parts when he met a mad explorer from Norway seeking two crewmembers to sail with him from Tierra Del Fuego to Antarctica. He told us about the insanity of the voyage there, and the causalities of the trip back. Luckily, he avoided becoming a casualty, opting out of returning with the explorer after witnessing the rage with which the captain wielded his arms and tightened his legs around the crow's nest of the mast during life threatening swells that seemed to only intensify the captain's lunacy.

Handing me the book to examine, I took it into my hands. I could almost feel the dampness it still carried from his journey across the ocean.
Years later, and oceans away I stood in front of my bookshelf packing for a family inspiration vacation. My father was turning sixty, and we were about to spend a week together as a family.

Intuiting the chaos of moments surely to come, I paused, and I swear, "I heard God laughing".

STITCH

I grabbed the book off the shelf, and nestled it into my backpack.

The book opened in moments that magnified love, and heightened laughter each day. It also served as a good reminder that the path continues unfolding wherever and whenever you show up with heart, and presence.

One morning, my father and I had taken off on one of our adventures, and found our way to an iconic café in Stuart, Florida. Before long, the gorgeous barista and I had made friends, and were engaged in conversation. Along the way, I happened to mention that I spoke Czech. She immediately turned to her colleague. "Mluvíš česky?" the colleague said in utter surprise (You speak Czech?). Our mouth's opened in foreign tongues; the moment began to grow wings, and we all seemed to fly away. Astonished by the instant jolt of excitement that had entered the room, we had obviously connected with spirit in the purest of its form, and re-entered a place both of us had been longing to find; Czech.

Again, "I heard God Laughing..."

Later that day, I was rinsing off sand from my feet near the ocean with my little brother. I thought of how synchronistic the encounter was that had taken place earlier that day. At that moment, I opened my phone to see one of my new friends had liked my Facebook page. Then suddenly I looked down into the grass, and saw a ten-dollar bill sitting there baking in the sun. I thought about the morning, the baristas, Czech, and my father. The girls insisted on buying our coffees. My father and I both left ten- dollar bills, and vanished out the door.

It seems the lesson is simple... whatever it is. And most definitely... God, he, she, is laughing... Eternally.

STITCH 008

Stealing Fire

"Make no small plans, for they have no magic to stir (wo)man's blood."

–Daniel Burnham

Daniel Burnham was the architect who, along with John Root, planned the World's Columbian Exposition in 1893, and is largely responsible for planning the rebuilding of Chicago after the fire of 1871. This phrase is painted on the wall of Midway International Airport above an elaborate set of maps that led to the building of the city so many of us love and adore. Passing by it countless times, I've bowed my head in praise attesting to the glory of these words. For like you, I have felt the magic stirring in my blood. Though the question so often becomes...

Where do we turn in the darkest hour just before the dawn? How do we summon the courage of Prometheus, and steel fire from the gods to bring light to our vision when we are suddenly cornered by darkness?

In this piece, we will be delving deep into the most powerful place in humanity; into the heart of hearts - into the glimpse -the vision; the emotion behind the motion, the step before the step. We will explore how crafting a vision begins with taking action from an inspired place that is uniquely yours – one that you define with what you decide to fight for in this life. Along the way, we will also be tying together themes of love, music, and heroism. We will be visiting stories about Alexander the Great, an Argentinean blues guitar player, and a version of yourself that you might be dying to reignite.

Ready?

A while ago a Greek friend of mine said, "Nathan, I want to tell you a story. It is the story of Alexander the Great and his rise to power." He continued, "There was a knotted-string, unfathomably complex and bundled. Many men tried to untie it, but

THE ARTISAN ENTREPRENEUR

none could even find a place to begin. The great Alexander stepped forward, drew his sword, and split the knot with his blade." My friend turned to me and said, "understand?" I nodded my head, and he broke into laughter.

I tell this story and think about what a shame it is that zen masters are often disguised as ordinary people who never know how important they truly are. Another Zen master took the shape of a legendary blues guitar player that I had the distinct pleasure of knowing during my time living in Argentina. He was passionate beyond words, and had enough strength in one forearm to hold the bottom string of the guitar all the way to the top of the fret board mid solo.

I remember a late night playing music with him when he muttered something to me that I will never forget. "Nathan... Tienes que dar todo por nada." This translates to English as, "You have to give everything and expect nothing." He then said, "My friend, we must be happy and celebrate tonight, for tomorrow, we will awake wiser."

As I tell these stories I am reminded of the core behind everything that we do, the heart: The wisdom of Alexander to take action when others would not, and the courage to do and to give for the sake of the principle of giving. To do otherwise is not truly giving, but dealing.

And now the question becomes: who are we in the face of adversity?

How often have you been living your life, building your dreams, and fighting the good fight, when suddenly you're invaded? The vision of life you've been dreaming up is suddenly threatened by an external force. Perhaps even by your own actions, or when the love of your life is suddenly at odds with you? What do you do? How do you act?

Well, this is where the greatest chapter begins. It is in this place, this perfect storm, that you become once again the person that she truly loves, and the hero that good people admire.

"For behind every good story is a love story..."

I've written about this in previous letters, and I will say it again. Picture yourself in a story. Your life is a book that you're reading. What do you want the main character to do? In the face of all adversity, who is it that the hero becomes?

STITCH

"Go get her..." you whisper to yourself, clenching the book and kicking the sheets. Though it is dark out, you are awake because there is one big truth that you can't ignore. Behind these pages is you. It's the hero in you – the one that lives in the stirring of your blood. And it is the version of yourself that has the power to sing your song of hope to the high heavens even in the face of all adversity, and win her back.

Win your dreams...

If a Trojan horse appears in your court, you must act.

Author's Confession:

I confess that when I wrote this I did not have the courage to say what I truly meant.

It was a time when I was still confused about what had happen in my process of becoming the integrated artisan entrepreneur; learning to do business, despite displeasing others.

I had a mentor who taught me about designing and manufacturing custom handmade eyewear. I worked with him for about one year very closely. Then when I wanted to create my own line, he exploded like a volcano. I was quite threatened by him, but knew I had to carry on with the vision of the product I was so eager to create. The burning desire to do so grew until a perfect set of circumstances aligned to give me the creative opportunity to make my own line of handmade glasses. I followed my intuition despite my eagerness to please him, and what resulted was an incredible line of handmade eyewear called the WalknTalk Visionaries.

In the moment before I was about to seal the deal with the manufacturer I called a mentor in Chicago who gave me a pep talk to go forward with my plan. In that moment, despite a lapse of emotional clarity, I found my center again, and acted from my core.

I knew that this product was going to help me reach the next level of revenue in my business, and solidify the product offering of my WalknTalk brand.

When I finally launched the product, the glasses were sold as sunglasses. They came with a beautiful leather case I created, and a cloth that had a peculiar image on it. It was a picture of the Chicago Skyline taken through the lens of a 1920's phoropter.

THE ARTISAN ENTREPRENEUR

I had discovered the beautiful apparatus as a child, and was always inspired by the inspirational value it carried. It made me think of perspectives, and trying on new ways of thinking.

I won a bid on Ebay to buy the relic with seven seconds to spare. When it arrived my photographer and I took it to the Metropolitan Club in the Sears Tower, and photographed the skyline through it with a focus on the John Hancock building; inspired by the ultimate visionary.

If you've ever worn glasses, then you would know the several different lenses that the optometrist uses to craft your perfect prescription.

The symbolism of the photo was meant to do the same. Instead of crafting your prescription, the image, and the product are meant to symbolize the crafting of an awareness —an inner visionary we are constantly fine-tuning inside of all of us.

 The idea behind the WalknTalk Visionaries thus is to use your experiences to craft your vision, and then everyday, when putting on your WalknTalk frames, to consciously put on your awareness of your visionary self, and empower the visionary in you.

Thankfully my filmmaking skills improved over the years, thanks to my good friend Ricardo who I met in Portugal. He and I created this special clip to highlight the WalknTalk visionaries shortly after in Sedona, Arizona.

Watch it here: http://visionaryframes.club

(See a photo of the visionaries, the cloth and the phoropter here:
https://www.walkntalk.com/collections/eyewear)

STITCH 009

Snapshot

"Autumn carries more gold in its pocket than all other seasons."

–Jim Bishop

Is it just me or are we all beginning to long for park benches, rustling leaves, and time with nature? Thus begins the time of reflection...autumn.

When nature reaches its height, leaves blaze with expression, and then they fall. It's like a symphony. The entire year, building, layering, sprouting, stringing. We are the conductors, and life is the music, always there in front of us the whole year-long. The lovely flowers, the plans and happenings of the year, and then suddenly in a flash, it's just a memory, a breaking wave on the shoreline.

A wise person once said, "Unpack your day carefully, and then carefully pack it back up before bed." But why?

Well, perhaps it has something to do with what Socrates said. "The unexamined life is not worth living." Well my friends, this year's not quite over, but one could say that a certain phase of it is. Farmers plan for harvest, teachers plan for exams, and businesses plan for taxes and budgeting. But what about us? What do we plan for?

This is a slow but sudden time of change, the shifting of summer to fall, and the inevitable trap of nostalgia that would be inhuman to avoid and unwise to overuse. That's right, nostalgia is a tool, and it has its place.

It's a feeling we earn, like the harvest. A sort of cider we drink. Healthy if it's fresh, and potentially intoxicating when fermented. Either way, it's something we can tap into, and use to enhance these moments that are just dripping with Vision. After all, the past is our greatest teacher, so long as we don't get stuck in it.

VISION. FEELING. GROWTH.

THE ARTISAN ENTREPRENEUR

Are you awake? Are you sure? Pinch yourself just to be certain. Many a play has been written, and many a song has been sung about the dream-like nature of life. Let's pause for a brief moment, and recall an earlier theme in this text's history.

"Live your life as if it were a novel, you the main character, living and writing each verse..."

Now imagine yourself on a park bench examining this past year, the year before, and so on. Do so as an old fashioned photographer would examine rolls of film for brilliant snapshots. Let the sounds, smells, and feelings of the fall open up a world inside of you, your world. The one where you go to follow your intuition to the place that predicts good and bad, foresees familiar circumstances, and then tacks like a salty sailor whose seen similar swells and knows now that it's nose first into the waves or capsizing into the night we go. Do you remember 15...? Ah... 15. Do you remember 18..?. ah... 18. How about 20? hmmm, and 21, yeah... Mistakes, excitement, brilliant circumstances, tragedies, sadness, pain, sorrow. 23.. a magical time.. then the inevitable collapse. The learning. The struggle. The breakdown. Spring time, and the breakthrough!
Does life not in fact have a rhythm? Is it not in fact telling a story? Are we not in fact the ones writing it with our thoughts, words, and actions? So a painter strokes the canvas, and the musician plays the song... What will we remember about this year? This year that showed us something new about life, about ourselves, and about what's possible... So what? How soon will we forget? Will we miss the fruits of this year by overlooking the potential of what could still be? Will a familiar force, voice, or person stay in our way? Or will we rise like doves, set out for the canyon, and take time to learn the tree line once more? Have the trees not grown? Have not we? Perhaps we're forgetting how strong we've become, that our horizons have expanded, and that wings could be there waiting and we wouldn't even know it. Indeed, chicks must nest before they can fly.

Think about it like this. Farmers grow apples all year just to make cider in the fall. Businesses work hard to generate revenue, create product, and then display it for one brief, beautiful, lit season we call the holidays. Now, what have you been doing this year? What has been unfolding? What vein of your life is expanding, and what would it take to let it bare a luscious fruit? Do you not deserve it? Are those snapshots you're

STITCH

finding of magic in your past not the results of split second decisions, unwavering conviction, and a willingness to see it through?

Now, what's the point of this exercise?

Well, need there be one? 21st century Philosopher, Alan Watts, says: "one doesn't make the end of the composition the point of the composition. If that were so, the best conductors would be those who played fastest, and there would be composers that only wrote finales, and there would be people that went to concerts just to hear one crashing chord" He goes on to say..."Dancing is not about aiming at one spot in the room to arrive at… the whole point of dancing is the dance."

What we should be curious about here is how can we get more out of this dance? Where else can we be dancing? Could traveling to somewhere to dance around for 2, 3, or 10 days feel like a lifetime when you look back on it? How couldn't it?

So often we reminisce past moments. Nostalgia knows... And, what does life feel like when we're dancing? Moving through the ballroom with purpose, joy, posture, elegance, and ecstasy - laughing until we cry - crying until we laugh - Is it not absurd? Absurdly beautiful! This song, this symphony, this invitation to move like Miles Davis's tune, Move. We live in an unprecedented age. One in which synchronicity seems to happen daily, and coincidence is almost always re-examined when it occurs. Why? People are noticing life in new ways. Perhaps they even have a new hunch about existence, about the intelligence of it.

Could it be that the old wives tales of fishing for an hour causing you to live two more could be true? Well, how couldn't it be? If you believe it, then isn't it so? And could sitting on a bench for 10 minutes, to write for 5 minutes about this year, this moment, and this life not cause you to realize something that could change the entire course of your existence? Well, how couldn't it? It's been proven, that small things are the one's that make a difference. Perspectives are the maps that events thus follow and flow from. So cheers, here's to life... I raise my glass of cider, to make a toast to you... To dancing ... here, there, and everywhere life takes us. For in the grand scheme, years can feel like lifetimes if only we have the courage to move, shake, and twirl, like those leaves that will soon be falling.

STITCH 010

Other Worlds

"We are what we feel."

–unknown

Have you ever imagined mapping the infinite milliseconds between the rising and falling of life's emotional rollercoaster? Or perhaps wondered what it would look like if that mapping was re-created with an untraditional measuring device? What if the way we've come to know the world could really just be a product of the instruments we've used to do so? And what if that all could be rearranged just by taking a step back to rediscover the senses we're employing to create these apparatuses?

I would like to open the door behind the response generators in our minds. The one located just beside the fuse panels, and next to the section in our brains labeled "world knowledge." Taking a step beyond, and into the "other worlds" section of the stacks, is where this lecture will continue. When you get there, feel free to take a seat. There is coffee, water, and tea. All of which are self-served and self-manifested. Simply think them into the cups you desire to consume them from before you.

Sound trippy? Good.

The "other worlds" section will feel like a trip. After all, it lives on a similar frequency of pure potentiality, but that's all I'll say, no need to rush ahead.

"With our thoughts we make the thing, by action we receive it."

-Wallace Wattles

We have all heard similar phrases of profundity stemming back to transcendentalists like Ralph Waldo Emerson who said "a (wo)man is what (s) he thinks about all day long." These profound formulations are equally thought-provoking, but what does it mean to actually think? What does it mean to wield the code of words comprised of letters sounds, and actions that we naturally compute all day long?

THE ARTISAN ENTREPRENEUR

The entry point into self-awareness begins with the word. As it says in the bible, "in the beginning, there was the word." The starting point of all creation is a statement; a "state" "meant". An intention placed into orbit of a "state, place, or way of being, that is created" with a sentence, "an entity sent".

They say that for every action there is an equal and opposite reaction; a mirroring effect that is created. Could it be that the digital age happening now and giving us things beyond our previous realm of comprehension is really just a direct reflection of the miracle that we ourselves actually are? Or the miracle of consciousness that we embody and employ? Is it modern artwork, showing us a different picture of the gears and levers already operating inside of us decorated with a different texture, material, and lifespan?

All of these questions can bring us deeper into our seats of self-awareness. However, the thought that can bring us there even faster is to think without thinking.
Try it for a second.

Go on.

Good, now where did your awareness go when it was forced to process something other than words?

Perhaps it went to your heart, and created an emotion? Or perhaps it went further into your brain. For those of you who went deeper into your brain, try to let go of the need to know for now, and just pretend that you're finally tall enough to get on the roller-coaster you always wanted to ride as a kid. Now, like an excited child, run past the gate. Get into the cart. Pull back the safety strap and hold on. That's it.

That's the excitement that will keep us always discovering.

Speaking of discovering, let us begin. Now again, think without thinking. Did you feel instead?

Good.

STITCH

What we have effectively done is touched the opposing entry points into awareness. One being "reason," and the other being "intuition." Now imagine they both live on a number line. At one end is reason, thoughts created with words. And on the other side, intuition, or thoughts created with feelings.

Now, back to our original question and our reason for even asking it – have you ever imagined mapping the infinite milliseconds between the rise and fall of our emotional states?

In this space of pure potentiality where you are currently seated, I am asking you to schedule the most important thing on your to-do list. There is one condition under which you must schedule it though. You must do it without time. Now look at your watch, pick up your pencils, or pull up your calendar be it digital or analog, and schedule the most important task you have on your mind.

Do it now.

Do you think I am kidding?

That's right. I forgot to mention. In this space where you are currently seated, there is no time. You are inside of the realm of pure potentiality. What you choose to do think or feel now will continue to occur. When? Now... Over, and over, and over again. Until that is of course, that you come back to this place and reset your task. My gosh, I know what you are thinking, "come all the way back here to change it?"

Back behind the response generators in our minds next to the fuse panels and into the section of the stacks labeled "other worlds". I know it seems like quite a distance... I never took calculus in school, but I heard the shortest distance between two points is a straight line. Would you agree? What if you decided to make this place a stop on your thought map or algorithm you're currently running in your brain?

Could it be that algo-rhythms are "something rhythms"? "Algo" in Spanish meaning "something". In my experience, most professors would call that a false association and definitely be perturbed. But the common individual on the other hand would most certainly be satisfied.

THE ARTISAN ENTREPRENEUR

Now, continuing with our metaphor... Have you ever heard of a blockchain? My friend happens to be an expert on crypto-currency and the other day was explaining what a blockchain is, saying roughly that "a blockchain is a series of algorithms computing to secure and confirm digital currency transactions between parties, and secured across a decentralized, distributed ledger."

Now, that being said, what if the carrying out of a decision were compared to a computing blockchain, and the speed at which our intellect created the thing on the other side of the computing algorithm was directly tied to the vibration of that rhythm.

Take for example the speed at which emotion moves through us. How about the emotion of confusion? How fast does it move? How about the emotion of love and ecstasy? How fast do they move?

Now think without thinking, and ask yourself which emotional speed and rhythm you would like to tie into your algorithm for making the most important decision and scheduling the most important task to be done without time. The strangeness you're most certainly experiencing in conducting this exercise is precisely like walking on the moon. Is it not? It is a feeling of rediscovery on many levels.

Millions of moments ago I worked in a pizza shop in downtown Chicago. Most days I spent engaging customers into the upward spiral of the present moment, and negotiating with the cooks to take out the deep dish pizza before the customers fell over famished from waiting. The cooks would always say, la vida es una lucha Natan. (Life is a struggle).

Never really liking this phrase, I deferred to a different sense of reason. Life is a not a struggle. Life is an equation, I thought.

When a girlfriend and I started dating she gave me a test of values to take. Upon completion we both discovered there to be a certain hierarchy that if followed and computed would equate to an experience of happiness together. Since following that equation we discovered moments when the equation creates happiness and moments when it creates sorrow.

STITCH

Could it be that all around the world, between every lover, family member, friend and foe there is an equation being computed? Could it be that its blockchain is just one "algo" rhythm away from creating a more satisfying currency? One that could "buy" us the break we so desperately long for, or afford us the space we so intensely feel that we need? What if once granted our satisfaction we then turned around and became satisfied from the granting of "it" to others? Would the world eventually become enlightened? And when that happened, would it then dance together look marching happy's in sync through life forever? Or would one person create a virus? And would that virus work, or would it just make our "algo" rhythm stronger?

Wherever you are. Whoever you're with. Behold the eye of the needle pulling the threads of awareness into your consciousness and ask can I afford not to "think without thinking" and not to "schedule time without time?" Is it not more exciting to live life by rediscovering it with a new sense of knowing each time we live it? To the infinite milliseconds of life and to the rapid creation of a deeper awareness with which to live it.

STITCH 011

Mojo De Mozart

"What lies behind us and what lies ahead of us are tiny matters compared to what lies within us. And when we bring what is in us out into the world, miracles happen."

-Henry David Thoreau

Have you ever considered thinking of your life as a symphony? As a winding river or stream with wide and narrow gaps in between?

Today I would like to take a moment to find peace, wherever we are. To ask the fundamental question, "what makes us happy?" And then with all of the courage and crescendo of Mozart, to be that, feel that, do that, and watch what happens.

A long time ago a special person introduced me to classical music.

He said "close your eyes sunny." He paused then continued. "Now, I'd like you to imagine your life, as a motion picture."

The music moved steadily in sync, and moments of my day passed through my mind like ripples through water.

It was in that moment that I recalled what my grandfather had said to me after hearing a choppy piece of music I had played on my guitar.

"Keep at it Nathan. One day playing your guitar will be just like walking through the park holding your girlfriend's hand."

While it may seem like these voices came from the same mouth, they did not. What I would like to imagine however, is that they came from the same mountain. Mountain?

THE ARTISAN ENTREPRENEUR

Yes, you know, as if that sound you hear when an elder breathes heavily, and then smiles with eyes that swell with moisture from the struggle of their speech is resulting from their trek up the mountain. All in an effort to give you that speck of gold dust they uncovered through the years.

Accessing the wisdom of their route is like summiting the mountain over and over. Until finally their eyes resemble the burning blue skies, and the twinkling dark nights they found on their path to this moment. And hopefully to the destination of peace and serenity that has found them.

The more I listen to the sounds of Mozart, the more life feels like a walk in the park. As if the "muse" inside of the symphony has the power to distill and purify every moment.

But how do we mute the minutia, and tune more directly into the muse of the symphony?

Well, that's the question that so many bold, and brave adventurers of truth have sought before us. One of those individuals, more contemporary than Buddha meditating under the fig tree, has a particularly unique, and simple recommendation.

Simply put he says "stay open." - Michael Singer, the Untethered Soul.

When life is loud, people are rude, and stress is steaming toward you like a freight train, "stay open," he says.

It's in these defining moments that we choose to either cut off our connection to source energy, or face the monster of the moment with love, joy, and outrageous acceptance of what is.

Approached in that way, he says that life becomes a game of leaning into the most perturbing situations with an open heart until every day we can see through the clouds, and feel the true touch of torrential rain as a child begging for attention pleading with us to dance when we are tempted to trudge.

Life is in motion, like the winding rivers and streams below the mountains. And according to a great book by Joel Olsteen "Peaks and Valleys" there is no need to

STITCH

worry for if we should ever forget, "life will take us down the mountain into the valley, and back to the winding rivers and streams to remind us."

In the states of beauty where we experience total love, peace, joy, and serenity we will always find the energy to go on, to build and become the masterpiece we are daily tempted to destroy, like slack in the halyards, we are invited to pull up, stay open, and harness the wind...to a moment that eclipses the sound of an emerging rhythm of spring.

"To observe... without judgment... beyond good and bad, life as beautiful..."

STITCH 012

Golden Leaves In Our Palms

"Nothing real can be threatened. Nothing unreal exists. Herein lies the peace of God."

-A Course in Miracles

Have you ever felt like you ordered the wrong thing off the menu, and then realized it was exactly what you needed? Like perhaps your deeper desire was only delayed a step in order to teach you to stop ordering what you don't want? Well, you're not alone.

This week I would like to turn our attention toward the perfection in the "apparent imperfection", and ask what is possible as we begin to build a heightened awareness around what we are choosing in our everyday lives.

Could it be that the reality we are wishing to manifest is actually stuck in a holding pattern just above us like planes waiting for an empty runway?

I ran into a friend in a cafe this weekend that proposed that thought about the planes. It's funny how metaphors find us exactly when we need them. They fall like golden leaves into our palms presenting the path to living the lives of our dreams. If only it were so simple to follow that path, wouldn't we all be living our dreams?

Well, who says we're not?

The question is, which dream? Yours or someone else's? Your better half's or the you, you thought you'd already mastered?

Rather than thinking this one to death, let's take a page out of our philosophy textbooks and remember that according to Nietzsche, "reason has been turned into a tyrant" governing every aspect of our lives.

THE ARTISAN ENTREPRENEUR

And isn't it true that we can drive ourselves nuts thinking too much?

So what's the alternative you might ask.

Well, "feeling" I suppose...

What if the answer to all life's quandaries was actually hiding in a bottle of wine? Not in the drinking of it, but in the composition of the drink. And the drinking of course as well, within reason. There is a philosopher that says that life should reflect the wine we drink. That we shouldn't live it purely rationally, but emotionally and irrationally as well. That we "discover life" through it's sensuality and sustain it through the use of reason; a collection of all of our senses. That to drink pure alcohol in order to feel a buzz would of course forsake the beauty and pleasure of savoring those tannins in a moment of pure bliss.

Am I suggesting you open a bottle of wine when feel as if you've made a wrong decision?

Well, perhaps, but not literally. What's being suggested through this direction is that exploring the irrational, the place where art and creativity lives and love for that matter, in fact leads to discovering the next pieces of the puzzle of life.

"Fill what is empty, empty what is full."

I ran into another friend two weeks ago in a different cafe who said this to me. It's a poetic notion, and one that makes sense as well. When you're at a loss for words, why not open a book and let some good ones find you? Or when you're teeming with love, joy, and inspiration, why not write a song and post it for others to enjoy? It has been said that life is a series of ups and downs. Thinking about this recently I realized that the screen at a hospital patient's bedside depicts life quite literally in this way. Think about how the screen looks when there's a straight line verses when there are ups and downs. Are ups and downs not an indication of being alive?

If anything, maybe we need to stop seeing the "downs" as "downs" but rather as places to hunt for treasure!

STITCH

So in the words of Mark Twain, may we "throw off the bowlines. Sail away from the safe harbor. Catch the trade winds in your sails." and "Explore. Dream. And Discover." (all the new places life is calling us to embrace!)

So find your treasure, leaning into the wind as the boat finds knots hiding in the angle it takes towards the sea.

STITCH 013

Conversations With Tom Sawyer

"Only those who keep going, can truly know how far you can go."

-T.S. Elliot.

Have you ever looked closely at something and felt like it changed from your gaze? If not an object, then perhaps a person? Or the reverse, have you ever been looked at, seen, or observed, and then felt suddenly changed or transformed? I would like to delve deep into one of the subtleties of transforming our awareness, and fine-tuning our sense of purpose in life: how it occurs, the sign posts, and what we notice.

One Monday afternoon I was punching out journals in the WalknTalk studio. Gazing out over the treetops, and observing the pearls of light on Lake Michigan. The air was heavy with wonder and question as I pondered an equation that felt like a labyrinth of possibility.

"When opportunity knocks, you take it." –Dr. Greg Reid

Just then I heard my phone ring. It was a friend from Prosperity Camp, a group I had attended on a whim in Palm Springs this year, and seemed to be altering the course of my career in a magical way.

"Call this guy, he has an extra ticket to the CUBS game today."

I read the text, and quickly realized possibility was presenting itself. The last thing I wanted to do was leave my workshop. When I get my head into something, I'm usually set on doing it, and this particular afternoon all I wanted to do was work, and write.

My head spun around as I thought for a moment. I then gazed at the porcelain frog in my bathroom, just like the one in my grandmother's house. I could hear her voice say, "all work and no play makes for a dough boy, Lovey."

THE ARTISAN ENTREPRENEUR

"Maybe it's a good opportunity to grab a view," I thought.

A view? Yes, a different perspective. I knew the gentleman I was being introduced to came highly recommended from an all-star friend of mine, and this was actually a golden opportunity disguised as a ballgame on rainy night.

I looked at my phone and called the guy up.

"Hello," he said.

We broke into a great chat about Prosperity Camp, our mutual friend, and life.

While the answer was simple, I still resisted.

"Gosh, you know, that sounds like a wonderful opportunity. I just have so much going on," I said.

"That's alright," He said.

I took a deep breath, and thought to myself. Just relax. The work will get done, and the story will get written. Opportunity is knocking at the door.

"Wait, you know what. I would love to go with you tonight if that's alright." "You bet, come on by whenever," he said.

"I'll see at a quarter to seven," I confirmed.

On the way over, I thought about a book I had been reading called Peaks and Valleys by Spencer Johnson. Coincidentally, my grandmother gave it to me two years before she passed. It seemed cliché and spent the first two years on the shelf before one day I discovered its value.

Feeling like now was a good time to pick it back up, I did. There is an old man that lives on a peak, and occasionally comes back down to the valley to chat with a young man that lives there. When the two are together, the boy discovers the peak, and realizes that "when you remember to apply what you learn on the peak while in the valley, you find a peak. And when you forget, well, you find a valley."

STITCH

I couldn't help but chuckle to myself as I pulled up to the gentleman's beautiful house, and felt like I was the character in the novel going to talk with the wise old man on the peak.

Appearing as if out of nowhere, he emerged from a sidewalk overgrown with tree limbs. His head bobbed up from under a branch.

"Hey, I'm Chuck."

An honest outstretched hand awaited me. I grabbed a hold of it.

"It's nice to meet you, Chuck. I'm Nathan."

We walked steadily toward the stadium. As we walked the rain came down, but neither one of us seemed to mind. Arriving to the box office, we picked up the tickets and swiftly made our way to our seats. The game was delayed, though our conversation seemed to have an early start. Bypassing the beer counter, hot dog stand, and the rest, we got straight into it.

I told him about my various projects, and the madness of everything I was working on, the stream of possibility that seemed to just keep pouring into my path, and the incessant propensity to keep it all moving forward.

"Wait," he said, "you write a story every week to two thousand people and it's called Tom Sawyer Tuesday."

"That's right, it's named after this journal, and while it doesn't always come out on Tuesday I do my best to get it out every week," I said.

He paused. "What if you started to think like Tom Sawyer with everything else you were doing?"

He told me about his daughter that went to a special type of school that welcomed student exchange. I told him I had coincidentally been invited to speak there a year ago. And that three years ago I met a teacher from the International School of Prague in a dark pub in Europe who invited me to talk with forty seniors in a senior advisement program.

THE ARTISAN ENTREPRENEUR

(See it at: walkntalknation.com)

"I feel like I'm doing all of this to tell a great story one day. But really, I have this feeling that I'm turning into a writer. The reason I started into business was to spread a message about personal growth through travel. Literally I was staining paper with coffee on my rooftop in Buenos Aires with a dream that one day the journals could WalknTalk. And now I feel like it's time to talk directly about the message. To encourage kids and people to learn languages, build niches abroad, and create yourself with a trip," I revealed.

"Well, maybe that's what you should do then Nathan," He said.

I looked off into the distance, not paying much attention to the score board.

"Say, we should take a picture, and send it to Todd," I suggested.

"Write him, 'freezing our asses off, wish you were here,'" Chuck laughed.

As we retired the night and said our goodbyes, a lightness flowed through my body. It was as if a weight had been lifted, and the confusion dispersed.

My mind wandered to the scene in a movie from the 1990s called Angels in the Outfield. I decided to re-watch it in my car. The trailer narrates, "they gave the world something to believe in."

"Just call me Al, no one can see me or hear me but you." "Why me?" the little boy asks.

"You asked for help. We come, we go. It's an as needed situation."

"I'm vapor. Keep your nose clean, and your heart open."

"The angels are out sunny. We'll be in touch."

A tear formed in the corner of my eye.

"That's true," I said to myself.

STITCH

Stepping out of my car, I grabbed my longboard from the backseat, and dared to ride all the way down from my fifth floor parking garage, something I had never attempted.

Smiling, screaming, and laughing, I made it to the bottom feeling like I'd just conquered a double black diamond on a ski slope.

The next day sitting up in the Sears tower stroking my keyboard, it hit me: "invite the good into your life with an open heart, and an open mind, and the rest will take care of itself."

Whether you're feeling alone, or confused on the rocky path of life. Remember to keep inviting the good people in, and to say yes when fear wants you to say no. After all, yes = success, eventually.

STITCH 014

Meeting Huck Finn

"Synchronicity: A meaningful coincidence of two or more events where something other than the probability of chance is involved."

-Carl Jung

Have you ever shocked everyone on the "L" train – even yourself? I have.

Imagine this, I'm sitting on the train in Chicago, sleeping, after a long day trotting around downtown, drinking wine, and networking – rough life, I know – next to my friend visiting from Prague, Czech Republic, when I suddenly awoke to a shocking site.

Across from me was a guy reading Huckleberry Finn. I perked up, and immediately said "Hey man, do you mind if I ask you a question?"

A few people looked up from their phones.

"I have this leather goods company called WalknTalk and I make leather journals. My most popular journal is the Tom Sawyer and I'd really love to know your definition of Tom Sawyer. Do you mind?"

The passenger was quite shocked, but very kind, and proceeded willingly.

"Well," he said. "He's adventurous. Enterprising. And takes life as it comes, I guess." "Dude, great description, really, thank you so much."

"Actually, I've seen you around campus, didn't you go to Loyola?" He continued, "I've actually seen your journals and I was thinking of buying one."

"Wow, thank you," I said. In my head, I thought, Seriously? You're kidding me.

THE ARTISAN ENTREPRENEUR

"Actually I just got a job in Colorado, and I'm heading out west soon. How much are they?"

"Well this one is made of Horween Leather from Chicago and it's seventy-five dollars, but the standard Tom Sawyers are forty dollars. I guess I could go forty on this one if you want."

"Sold," he said. "But I don't have cash."

"No worries, I can take a card."

I ran his card, and a minute later we both arrived at our stop. We got off the train and disappeared separately into the night.

My Czech friend trailed behind in disbelief.

"Magic, Nathan" he said squeezing my shoulder.

I laughed. "I don't know what to say. I guess it's a Tom Sawyer thing."

STITCH 015

Number Lines

"Numbers rule the universe." -Pythagoras "With our thoughts we make the world."

–Buddha

Do you remember those long dreamy days in math class as a kid learning about number lines? Well it turns out they weren't all a total waste.

According to a friend of mine, number lines are life's greatest gift to understanding who we are, and who we choose to become in the world. Let's close our eyes to the mundane, and re-examine life's possibilities with a keener sense of how we got here in the first place.

I would like for you to imagine the house where you grew up. Think about it in great detail. Close your eyes and envision what it was like before you arrived, prior to your birth. Now, think about the motion of how you came to be. Your Mom pushed, your Dad cheered, and the doctors played catch as you were delivered.

There is a famous German philosopher who talks about this idea of being "thrown into the world". For years I've thought about it, and wondered. Can we not just throw ourselves back into the world? And is the very nature of intending, and then manifesting not a totally parallel process to being born?

It's like a child playing with a slingshot in the back woods. Finding a pebble, putting it in the sling, pulling it back, and then letting it fly. Recently I returned from a trip to San Diego. It was there that I was walking down by the ocean with a friend I'd met years ago. You might remember him from a previous chapter as the guy I met on the train that put me in touch with those running the conference in Palm Springs. He said, "Nathan, everything we do in life is likable to a number line. If we think we're a -3, and we make five points of progress, we'll be at +2. And if we see ourselves as a

+5, and make five points of progress we'll be at a +10. It's all about semantics," he said.

"Semantics?" I asked.

"Yes, life is created with the words we craft it with..." he replied.

I started to reflect on prior trips to other countries. The intentions I set, the friends I'd made, the perspective I'd gathered, and the languages that I'd learned. A light bulb went off.

"Semantics...that's it!" I thought. Ever since I learned the Czech language I'd been thinking off and on in Czech, and then in Spanish, and also in Portuguese. Inherent in each of these languages is the culture, and a sense of bias about what is the nature of possibility with relation to everything in life. Language is steeped in mentality. Even in English, there are different terminologies, vocabularies, and ways of speaking that either limit or expand one's relationship to possibility.

I would like for us all to take a quick look in the mirror, and imagine what would be possible if we rearranged our number lines. What would life look like if we took a brief moment to throw ourselves into a space of possibility that had the potential to challenge us to think on a deeper level about who we are and who we are destined to become. At the Prosperity Camp in Palm Springs we did this. Observing other people that have created massive success, and made a huge difference in the world was awe- inspiring. But what was more, was the simplicity of the formula.

It seems that just by observing the "being" of those individuals, and where they saw each other on their own number lines was key. Perhaps it's time to take out a piece of paper, draw a line, and then commit to always seeing ourselves higher up on our own number lines than we give ourselves credit for being. It's that "being kind to your mind," and that never-ending sense of adventure in life that allows us to continue creating the possibilities we long to live with.

At the end of the day, the longing for something means that it must exist. Our quest in life is to stand up, and go find it. And when it is nowhere to be found, close our eyes, and create out of thin air.

STITCH

After all, isn't that how each one of us was created in the first place? Cheers to the freedom to follow the spirit, and create life as we see fit. As free spirits and visionaries, would we have it any other way?

STITCH 016

All in

"The one who moves mountains begins by moving small stones."

– Confucius

Have you ever woken up a couple thousand miles away, and thought, "oh my gosh, what just happened?"

I have this hunch that this mini panic is a siren waking us up at a deeper, inner level. It's as if the sound of the siren is only detectable once removed from our mundane every day existence of the routine. I'd like to explore this siren, and the art of listening to the world around us for clues. Realize that there are allies in this world and we find them when we step out in the direction of our intuition aligned with our higher purpose. There are people who want to assist you in building a life of purpose, and often moments of synchronicity that bring it all into focus.

After all, "hindsight is 20/20" as they say...

What we are pointing toward here is a strategy of how to develop a laser sharp focus, and a guiding intuition in crucial moments of choice, chance, and chaos.

The following story will feel like snapshots into present and past realities; mine and those of others at these critical times. We will be drawing from the following figures: A shooting coach for the Pistons that teaches finesse and visualization, a gaucho in Argentina that hitch-hikes to Antarctica, a life coach in Chicago that follows a Facebook ad west, and his buddy Nathan who, by chance, meets him on the beach in San Diego on his way to a bike conference in Las Vegas that he heard about a day earlier.

Call it crazy.

THE ARTISAN ENTREPRENEUR

The ability to follow a moment of inspiration – a thought that occurs in an instant in the form of a "crazy plan" – and then the recognizing of the fear that follows, and the taking of action anyway.

Years ago I started working with a life coach named Dave. He taught me about distinguishing being, creating clarity, and empowering decisions. If we want to get really good at being laser sharp in our pursuit of happiness, we need to recognize that it is in the subtleties that the magic is created.

Before you can hit three point shots you need to create a form and a focus that will attract the swoosh. A great teacher and shooting coach for the Pistons once drilled us at basketball camp, before we would even look at a hoop, Coach Steve would line us up. With one hand behind our backs, and facing forward, he would say: "ONE, get ready. TWO, platform. THREE, rotation." In these three steps, we would focus on our posture, set the intention to shoot, and then release the ball with a finesse watching it rotate up into the air.

TAKING BIG CHANCES=TELLING BIG TALES

In college on study abroad I was visiting a ranch in Argentina when I met a kindred spirit. He was a gaucho giving tours of Argentine folklore in Spanish, French, and English. He was worldly, and caught my attention immediately. We hit it off, and our conversation found a quick and certain depth, that just foreshadowed the beginning of an interesting friendship. He planted a verse from an 14th century poet in my mind, and walked away. He said, quoting Hafiz, "learn to recognize the counterfeit coins that will buy you a moment of pleasure, but then drag you for days like a broken man behind a farting camel."

As the day's festivities were ending I walked off toward the tour busses. Over the loud speaker a voice called out "Nathan... Keep it real brother." A few days later I get an email written in a sort of Shakespearean prose. It was the gaucho speaking to me in his endearing way. Enchanted by the note, I followed suit in my response.

Nine and a half months passed before my return to the ranch.

One day I realized I had to see him again. Two close friends and I drive there and find him in the back of the ranch saloon on break between announcing festivities.

STITCH

We embrace and he invites us all over to his mother's house that night for wine. When we arrive, we sit down in his living room and he begins telling us the story of how he built the house himself. I pointed to an interesting pillow on the couch to ask where it was from. He paused.

"Inside that pillow is a sleeping bag that I used when I hitch-hiked to Antarctica. You see I was traveling through a small town in Patagonia called Rio Gallegos when I ran into a Norwegian explorer. He had just crossed the Atlantic, and needed two crew members to make the sail to Antarctica. His former crew abandoned him claiming he was insane.
His boat was only twenty-five feet long. I knew that if I went, I would live a life-changing adventure. If I stayed, I would regret it for the rest of my days. It turns out he was crazy, and I decided not to return to South America on his ship. The voyage through stage 9 storms was too much for anyone to handle. I returned on a cruise liner. When I arrived, we got word his ship had sunk, and his next two recruits died. He miraculously survived. It's crazy I know..."

My friends and I stared blankly as our minds were somewhat blown by his heroic tale.

"I wouldn't change a thing though," he said.

CHOOSING WHAT YOU WANT = LIVING A GUILTY PLEASURE

A few weeks ago Coach Dave passed me on his bike in Chicago. He circles back, and tells me this story: "My house purchase fell through. I took it as a sign and thought about how I always wanted to move to southern California. I got in touch with an old friend on Facebook. She added me to a new-age-y group on there. Thirty seconds later, I saw a wanted ad for a live-in position in Cali in a mansion as a rehab coach that has experience with addiction. I message the guy. We hit it off. I flew out there to check it out. Came back to Chicago, and said 'nope. It's over. Moving to San Diego."

Dave saw a view into a parallel reality, took aim, and fired himself in the direction of his dreams.

In Chicago he lived on the beach, and already led a dreamy life living in one of the Northside's neatest old resort buildings with a private beach.
He wind-surfed in the

summers, and longboard surfed in the winters with a wet suit and icicles freezing on his face. He decided it was time to live more days on top of his surf board, and less days freezing in winter dreaming about summer. (www.davekehnast.com)

Witnessing Transformation First Hand

REINTERPRETING CHAOS= TAPPING INTO SYNCHRONICITY

Sometime after that, I had the pleasure of standing on the cliffs of DEL MAR with Dave at 101 11th St. Beach. I had texted him saying an Inspiration Vacation swelled up like a wave out of nowhere, and somehow I was riding it straight into San Diego: "Yeah, I was in Sedona with my Portuguese pal filming a video about being a Visionary to feature the new sunglasses when he and his girlfriend invited me to drive with them west to San Diego for a concert. I had already signed up for a personal growth oriented workshop in Chicago this weekend, but then I just thought well, perhaps this trip is a golden opportunity to go West again. So I did. Believe it or not I walked into a bike store yesterday, and the owner asked me if I was going to the National bike conference in Las Vegas next week. I told him I wasn't, but perhaps now I will be."

It was then that I was present to the possibilities of selling our wooden bikes there. I did some math and thought about rearranging my flights again. This is crazy, I thought to myself, crazy, but the opportunity to meet a lot of people in the bike industry was golden. I rebooked my flights on miles, and got a few deals.

"Looks like I'm going to Vegas on Wednesday – crazy isn't it?" I said to Dave. We were pulling off our clothes. Dave was putting on his wetsuit, and the both of us were just amazed by the present moment. The sound of the ocean was such a brilliant white noise. It reminded me of that siren.

"Man this is like the beginning of an incredible novel," I said to Dave.

"More like the end of one," he said.

"Yeah, if anything it just goes to show how close our dreams really are."

STITCH

"Yeah man, it's all about getting really clear about what you want, empowering choice, visualizing and taking action. It's funny there's a box of stuff I left in Chicago that I was going to send. I don't even need it now," Dave said.

I grabbed my GoPro and followed Dave on his surfboard into the ocean. Maybe this is the beginning of a film or something.

STITCH 017

Embracing Aha

"Your heart knows the way. Run in that direction."

-Rumi

Have you ever wondered if it's real? The magic of possibility aligning with divine time, and the realization of a dream coming true? And the bumpers that magically appear in the bowling alley of life to keep your dream on track when you sometimes find your head spinning?

I would like to explore the mystical moments that often occur as spontaneous circumstances aligning to give you that brilliant "aha", and clarity you need. More specifically, the ones that formulate out of events construed by things beyond your wildest imagination.

I suggest "belief" holds the key to unlocking these moments; the knowing that the next sign is coming on life's autobahn of the big dreamer's highway; the pie in the sky moments that tell you when to pull over, look up, and reach out to greet the man standing there holding the toll ticket to carry you onto your next exit.

Belief, "being the leaf," open, light, and free to go with the flowing prairie wind.

One week, while traveling back from a momentous trip to New York, riding the prairie winds, I stopped for some Amish pies and a chat with my good pal Marian. He is the father of five and has the voice of a mountain. Whenever we talk it seems our conversations are short and sweet, true and honest, like the day is long and the work is hard.

"Well that sounds good to me now Mr. Nathan," he always says.

THE ARTISAN ENTREPRENEUR

Feeling as if I was speaking merely rhetorically this visit, I made room for a few long chuckles, and told him how nice it was to see things going well. Walking out of his shop, and closing the door, it occurred to me that one of the things he said was a Pinterest quote I read last week.

"Success is rented, and it's due every day."

Thinking of his daily regiments of rising to shine early to do the work by day, eat pies by afternoon, and count stars by night, I realized the perfect simplicity in the system of his life. I also realized that he might be evolving his perspective on the use of technology, but that is no surprise to me because he is quite a savvy lad. And speaking of savvy lads, the Irish know how to prop you up when you're struggling to see the road you're walking.

"Do they?" you might ask. They do.

Walking to the restroom in a classy, Chicago mainstay two days later I heard the ramblings of two Irish lads and made an introduction.

A rumble of laughter followed as they signaled for me to join them and their wives at their table. The next day they were visiting me at the Metropolitan Club overlooking the windy city skyline.

In those precious moments not only did I learn that bartenders should never pour Guinness in a frosted mug, but that my Irish veins went deeper than I had realized.

They began telling me old Irish fables. Stories about storytellers, the likes of who they said I reminded them. Flattered, I continued telling them the story of Big Murphy, my great grandfather who I'd recently started a brand about.

As soon as I'd shown them a photo and mentioned the date 1916, they were intrigued.

"You do know that's an important date for the Irish now don't you Nathan?" they asked. I confessed I knew little of it at the time, and that 1916 was the year my great grandfather graduated from Syracuse Law. I scrolled down further to show them the 100 Years Collection of bags and belts.

STITCH

"You do know we just had the 100 year celebration in Ireland now don't you Nathan?" Bernadette said. My smile grew wider as each detail began ironing itself out to perfection.

"We did mention that we both have beautiful daughters you know, Nathan. Fine Irish girls."

I blushed, and told them how lovely they must be. A bellowing cloud of laughter seemed to ignite the already roaring pub-like conversation we had cocooned inside the jazzy sophisticated culture of the Metropolitan Club. "You'll have to excuse me as I go snap a few photos of the view before I go off to heaven," Jimmy said. And like that, the banter continued like a big band playing to the tune of long lost friends gathering for a pint.

As we said our goodbyes, an empathetic "thank you" repeated from my lips, and echoed from my heart. They seemed to have swept me up into a moment of great repose. A retreated sense of trust that everything was on track. One that left me there to ponder their uncanny arrival, and seamless departure from my world of "big thinking, big Murphy creating, dream-chasing pursuits." On one hand, I felt like I'd just met a few guardian angels, and on the other that perhaps it was all just a dream.

Whatever the case, I prefer to see life as a quest for recognizing moments that only the magic of trust, belief, and patience can draw into reality and paint on the canvas of our lives.

Keep inviting the charmers into your life, until you can clearly see that everything aligns.

STITCH 018

Your Powerful Monster

"Everyone has talent; what is rare is the courage to follow the talent to the dark place that it leads."

-Erica Jong

Have you ever created a monster? Worked your fingers to the bone, your brains to the limit, and your soul to the precipice of life? Great! Me too.

It is incredibly interesting to explore all of the places we get stopped on our journeys to building our creations, and the great lessons we can take from holding on tight right as they take off.

One day I was walking through the ballroom in the 1920s building I had just moved into on the waterfront in Chicago. A few people in the building were watching an old Frankenstein movie gearing up for Halloween. A friend shouted, "come on over and drink some wine with us Nathan." Thinking about all that I had left to do that day, I was very reluctant, but then eventually realized it to be the only sensible thing to do: relax.

He waived me over, and scooted aside to make room for me to sit; pinned between he, his girlfriend, and the armrest of the couch. With a sweet child-like smile he offered me a big bowl of popcorn, and poured me a generous glass of red wine. The lights around the ballroom garnished with black and orange ribbon intertwined between old candlelight fixtures made it feel like we were sitting on a set cut out from the film.
"What's the name of this movie?" I asked.

"Young Frankenstein," he whispered. My eyes grew bigger as the black and white screen grew wider. Hunched over a bowl of popcorn, and holding a glass of wine, my mind did something it doesn't do very often... it slowed down. Observing the peculiar

THE ARTISAN ENTREPRENEUR

Dr. Frankenstein, I took notice of the madness stewing within him. I could relate to his obsession to bring his creation to life.

Working with his assistant Igor and his lover Inga, the doctor grew restless as his various attempts to bring his Frankenstein to life seemingly failed. His efforts mounted into a frustration that only success could collapse.

"From the very first day when filthy bits of slime crawled out of the sea and called to the stars 'I am man,' our greatest dread has always been the knowledge of our mortality. But tonight, we will hurl the gauntlet of science into the frightful face of death itself. Tonight, we shall ascend into the heavens! We shall mock the earthquake! We shall command the thunders and PENETRATE THE VERY WOMB OF IMPERVIOUS NATURE HERSELF!" – Young Frankenstein

The Doctor continued ranting, demanding his creation to awaken, and move with the life force of the bolts of lightning he now commanded. Failing to awaken the giant the doctor hung his head slipping into a funk over a dinner plate.

"You haven't even touched your food Dr. Frankenstein" said Inga.

"Here, now I'm touching it, are you happy now?!" the doctor replied smashing his hands down on the plate. Gazing up at the ceiling the doctor sighed. A moaning noise came from below. Igor, Inga, and Frankenstein all looked at each other before the doctor lunged for the door leading into his laboratory. Scrambling to check on the monster on the table, the doctor, exalted, began opening the metal brackets containing the beast. The beast moaned.

"Whose brain did you put in him?" the doctor insisted.

"Err... Abby something..." Igor replied.

"Abby who?" said Dr. Frankenstein.

"Abby... Normal. Yes that's it, Abby Normal!"

"Are you saying that you put an abnormal brain in a 7 foot tall, 54 inch wide GORILLA!!!???"

STITCH

The plot continues unfolding with new sets of challenges all threatening Dr. Frankenstein's credibility as a scientist, and also the success of his creation. While at first it seemed even impossible for the 7-foot man to move, it later becomes a question of if he can be stopped at all. The movie moves with a cadence similar to the rhythm of everyone's life who has ever fully committed to following a dream.

While Dr. Frankenstein spent every waking moment developing a plan to pour all of his strength and sinew into, the resurrection of his precarious creation, he was then also obligated to see to that his creation be tamed with the rhythm of reason. With one last test he attempts to transfer some of his brain cells into the beast, and while nearly killing himself in the process, succeeds in doing so.

They say that often we need to literally be willing to give it all up, and lay it all on the line, and even die before our dreams come to life.
As a good friend of mine, Craig, says "it's okay to die, just don't hurt your body."

According to Alan Watts, deep down we all have our own fair share of "irreducible rascality." A part of us that would provoke our grandparents to call us "little devils" or "rascals" (or "brutes," as my grandmother would call me).

Knowing that this slice of mischief is actually the quintessential piece to igniting our brilliance, and literally turning everything we touch into gold with just a sliver of our efforts like fractals of the Philosopher's Stone, we must do everything and anything to preserve this cunning.

It's in this ungraspable concept that the smaller the object, the greater it's potential. The sharper the focus, the clearer the image. The higher we fly, the smaller we feel.

No matter where we are, ever, we are always just one thought, feeling, and emotion away from "it".

IT. . . the genesis of life itself.

In so far as we are concerned, the "crazy you" is the only you. Stay wild. Stay focused. Build your Frankenstein, no matter what.

STITCH 019

Theatrical Self

"However many languages you know, so that many people you are."

-Czech Proverb

This is a two-tiered message about being the painter then observing what has appeared on the canvas and guiding it into a masterpiece.

You will also notice the introduction of a concept I will illustrate that will hopefully highlight the creative force that exists in all of us, so that we can name it, claim it, and draw it out willfully.

A decade ago I began working on my godfather's one-hundred-year-old wooden sailboat in Rochester, New York. He taught me about the labor of love and sparked a passion in me for seeing the boat as a metaphor for life. As the years went on, we weathered storms, fixed leaks, and soaked in many steamy afternoons in the boatyard coupled with cruises on the Genesee river and Lake Ontario. The spirit of that place and those days coated my heart with an indelible layer.

Before long the "boatyard dogs" (my nickname for the men there) gave me a nickname as well; Picasso. For whatever reason it stuck. They would use it endearingly, but also to poke fun at my "look" and "dress." Such hypocrites – old hippies, bald and less ballsy, forgetting their big-hair-don't-care moments (with all due respect).

But what's my point?

Well, out of that place, and those characters arose a character in me. And how many characters do we all have inside of us? Several... And how often do we tell stories with a passion that certain people get and others have no clue what we're talking about, but nonetheless smile and acknowledge our passion?

THE ARTISAN ENTREPRENEUR

It is said that we draw from influences in our lives for years into the future. Even brief moments that occur in an instant, and then somehow stay with us forever like a bottomless pal of paint always chumming along waiting for us to get out the brush and draw upon them. And how do we get out the brush? Great question. We draw ourselves into the present and call on the character within.

I'd like to take a moment to introduce that character as the "theatrical self." It's the part of us that we reflect on, recall as happy, brilliant, passionate, loving, full, foot loose and fancy free, and above all ALIVE. It is also the big hair don't care part of us - the free, expressing, doing, not over thinking, being, and not worrying, self. By the way, it is also the extendable link in our chain of possible selves that we always have the freedom to continue growing, expanding, and creating.

Now, why does any of this matter? Well, you tell me. Who is the person painting this summer? What buckets of paint are most prevalent, and why? Where are those buckets, those colors, and those paints that really make this whole canvas something that gives us pause and tickles our feet to dance?

If you're looking for a place to find them, I suggest you stand barefoot on the hot sand until you stop thinking, start running, and jump into the water with your best big hair don't care smiling face, yawping Whitman, and grinning Sherlock expression. And when you come up for air, in that moment when your beautiful face graces the surface once again with your real presence, there will be your pals, buckets, and all the castles you could ever dream of building.

See you at the beach, because life's too short not to build a few castles.

STITCH 020

Wisdom From The Galaxy

"And whether or not it is clear to you, no doubt the universe is unfolding as it should."

-The Desiderata

We must gaze into the stars…

Not just the ones out there in the galaxy, but those surrounding us, in the media, the neighborhood, and right here in front of the mirror.
The following inspiration flows from an observation that requires a deep dive, a long rope, and a lot of courage to connect the outer evolving reality with the inner intricate self.

How might we go about tying such a knot? Well, so glad you should ask. With the audacity of resorting to our 8th grade education and a poem I discovered in the most magical bookstore in Chicago.

Well, time to jump. No nose-plugging. Let's go.

I woke up from the daydream I was having some time ago sitting on the beach overlooking Lake Michigan. I had been contemplating my calendar and predicting somewhat of a Big Bang approaching in August with the looming string of events slowly but surely roping me in.
Each event had a "larger than life" quality, the type of stuff that usually takes place over the course of two months, was about to happen in a four-day stint. To be clear, I wasn't getting married, but I was somewhat married to the idea of doing everything that was on my plate.

It was as if the stars were aligning with a mission to collide. But isn't that what they do? I thought to myself. Collide and create. That day, a friend of mine and I were having lunch. At one point he turns to me and says, "do you ever wonder about space? I find it just fascinating imagining how far light travels." Later on, out of the blue he says, "you know Nathan, I think you're on the right path."

THE ARTISAN ENTREPRENEUR

That's reassuring I thought, despite feeling exhausted from a week of sheer madness. It was in that moment that his phone beeped. It was a CNN update about the Olympics. "I am just loving this coverage," he said. We sighed for a moment, and made our way back into a brilliant conversation. An hour or so later I sat down to write, and began connecting the dots. I looked out over the city I love so much, and noticed it teeming with energy from the sun. I thought about all of these hot summer days, the boiling moments sweating through the avenues, the athletes lunging toward success, and the human race advancing the story of 2016 one day at a time.

I think what I was feeling in that moment of collision is one of the ingredients in this word we call grit, and the reason why we need the Big Bang to happen in our lives. To build grit, and succeed when our past selves might have failed. At times, life is very full, and the only way out is often through the eye of the storm. I thought to myself about what another friend had recently said about integrity. "Thoughts, words, and actions." He mentioned something about noticing where these three are or are not lining up in our lives.

I realized I'd done the right thing by going through with this week's hectic schedule. I realized, I would never have to say what if, and that would make Mr. Mark Twain a happy man, as he himself said: "Twenty years from now you will be more disappointed by the things that you didn't do than by the ones you did. So throw off the bowlines. Sail away from the safe harbor. Catch the trade winds in your sails. Explore. Dream. Discover." –Mark Twain

As I planned to head home that day, I was reminded of a book waiting on my shelf. It's one I read every now and again when I seek the wisdom of the stars, and their subtle ways of aligning, often for a greater purpose usually just beyond the horizon. It's called the Desiderata.

STITCH 021

You Are The Gold

"You are the gold they are three feet from."

–Craig Collins

Have you ever noticed how the outer focuses the inner? How the foundation of mind is based in the space through which it flows and vice versa?

This idea plays into a bigger process of transformation as we move in the direction of our dreams, literally.

One week ago, while driving over two thousand miles from Chicago to San Diego passing rivers, mountains, and valleys, I noticed a shift in my being. As if the places I was driving through were somehow driving me. Trekking through the Rockies in Colorado, and stopping for gas, a big sign read "Idaho Springs." Wandering a bit further down a snow dotted highway, I pulled over to enjoy the mountain air, a coffee, and a view. Looking up at the mountain I noticed another sign, "ARGO Gold Mine and Mill."

"Ha," I laughed. It just so happened I was heading to a conference being put on by a man named Greg Reid, the author of a New York Times bestseller called "Three Feet from Gold." Calmly acknowledging the synchronicity of the event, I continued through the Rockies, down into Utah, and through the desert. The mountain scape seemed to awaken a force within. The road like water began cleansing my mind, and freeing up space.

"The ordinary is not ordinary, it is extraordinary, uncanny" -Heidegger.

Engaging a new rhythm of life is something that happens naturally when you change the life around you. According to a book called the The Path of Least Resistance by Robert Fritz, the creative energy in our lives is something that can be harnessed through observing, and copying the way mother nature does so. About this, Kevin
M. Roddy says: "He argues that just as wind moves around natural obstructions,

seeking the path of least resistance, so do we attempt to move around the structures of our lives--getting by with as few hassles as possible. Fritz's advice is to modify the structures, enabling the creative energy within to flourish instead of dissipate."

At the conference, several distinguished authors, inventors, and movers and shakers presented on related themes. Among them was Gene Landrum, the founder of Chuck E. Cheese, who advocated a philosophy of self-creation through creatively destroying the current version of ourselves. "Creatively destroy yourself in order to powerfully re-create yourself, "he said, "Ask yourself: what would the life I am currently living look like if I was surrounded by blank everyday?" (Mountains, rivers, skyscrapers, desert, foreign languages, farm land, etc.)

Whatever you're yearning for could be the structure necessary to channel yourself more deeply into your own vision. How would changing what we feel, see, and observe change how we feel, see, and observe? And what would be possible once that shift would occur? Could life suddenly be lived on an entirely new trajectory? Could catapulting ourselves into this transformative reality change it all on a quantum level? And could it do so in record time?
Noticing that time passes differently on the road, I set out to understand why. It seems that speed + stimulus = potential to be more fully engaged in the present moment.

Thinking with my hands curled over the wheel flying through the Rockies, I pondered. Naturally my mind moved to Einstein's theory of relativity. Recalling a book I had read years ago called Einstein's Dreams by Allen Lightman, I thought of a brilliant point that was made. He explores the speeding up of time through the lens of a love story. Showing the two lovers so drawn into the present moment, he illustrates how they live years of experience in just hours, and feel only minutes have passed. The stimulus of being drawn into the present is so powerful that it shifts us into a new orbit.

Imagine falling in love.

When two lovers meet, time suspends for a brief moment, and soon perfect strangers become an inseparable pair. This is the effect of openly moving in the direction of our dreams. Allowing the mountains, rivers, and streams to reprogram us. It is having the courage to powerfully shift into the slope like a snowboarder dropping into the

STITCH

powdered mountain, and decidedly carving a path. Moving with the mountain means unapologetically moving forward into the unknown. Anything short of commitment in such phases of transformation can mean certain derailment and destruction. It is in these moments that "We and only We" must decide for ourselves.

A friend of mine, Todd Thompson, has a great adage. He says, "If you want to make God laugh, just tell him your plans."

And I say, tell anyway. Tell your story. Speak your truth, and through your own discernment listen for the pitch of laughter that harmonizes with the ditty in your heart. Life is a song, and great songs have qualities of a symphony. They build and fall, and build again. Moving with the landscape of life like birds through the woods tracing the river. So much of re-creating ourselves seems to be buying the ticket, and taking the ride. The key ingredient for success in any of those trips is the courage to powerfully discern the message we're receiving, and commit.

STITCH 022

Being Bold

"Be Bold and Mighty Forces Will Come To You."

–Goethe

Can you recall the first time you realized you had something extraordinary to share with the world? Or if unsure of what that something is, at least a notion that somewhere in your midst is lingering a great secret about yourself, that if given time is bound to bring to the world something of great value?

In this chapter, I would like to introduce one of my secret, visionary techniques. This technique is one that has always helped me make real the path ahead. Oddly enough it came through an encounter with a stranger I met on a train three years ago that muttered a phrase that I will never forget. It is the title of my secret Pinterest board, and the mantra I tell myself whenever I need a boost.

"It's mine. It's out there. I deserve it. I have a purpose for it, and that purpose will help and heal the world." –Stranger from the train

As I was walking through Chicago a week after learning this phrase, I saw a family passing by. There was a little girl wearing a t-shirt that said "don't wish for it, work for it."

When I was a kid, I wore a shirt and tie to school everyday and prided myself on my double-Windsor knot, otherwise known as the "vicious v." Perhaps it should have been called the "virtuous v." The school was strict, and inspired allegiance to the code "men for others." Since then I've always known that my job was to create my job. I wanted to talk with lots of people, and speak other languages. My first business card even said, "Help the world. Be positive."
Somewhere along the way, I realized that's everyone's job.

It wasn't until I was caddying one day for Tiger Wood's swing coach's brother Craig Harmon, that I realized "it's not what, but how."

THE ARTISAN ENTREPRENEUR

Mr. Harmon asked me, "Nate, what do you want to be when you grow up?"

"Not sure," I told him. "All I know is that I want to build my life, and be the designer of my existence."

On a separate occasion on the golf course, this time playing with a group of guys I had never met before, I remember meeting one man with four business cards. Wait, he has four companies? I thought, wow... That's interesting. Is that even possible? There are moments in our development that we never forget. Let's just call them seeds in the garden of our mind. They are as perennial as tulips in spring, and they are there for a reason.

STITCH 023

Stranger On The Train

"Intuition is the whisper of the soul."

-Jiddu Krishnamurti

Three years ago I was boarding that Amtrak train in Chicago. A voice from behind me called in a friendly tone, and said: "hey there, you seem like an interesting person. I'd love to know your life's story. Feel free to come sit with me for a bit."

It was dark, and the diesel tint in the air was heavy. How strange, I thought to myself. The guy seemed so friendly, but then again it was late, dark, and I had a ton of valuables that I needed to keep an eye on.

In the morning, I went to the dining car for coffee. It was a gorgeous sunny day, and the passing countryside was somewhat of a dream I stepped back into. I started chatting with an Amish fellow and told him about WalknTalk.

Before I knew it, there was that gentleman from the night before. His face, almost angelic, was soft like his voice, and in an instant, I knew we were meant to meet. In one hour, we formed a bond that has grown into an incredible friendship. We became Skype pals, and partners in crime discussing the intricacies of life, vision, and coincidence. One day I was sitting around the WalknTalk studio when I got a call from him. "There is something I want you to write down," he said. "It's mine. It's out there. I deserve it." He paused. "Got it?" he said, "Good, now the second part. It's mine. It's out there. I deserve it. I have a purpose for it. And that purpose will help and heal the world."

Since that day, I decided to empower those words.

Ready for my Secret Visionary Technique?

THE ARTISAN ENTREPRENEUR

Okay, brace yourself. It's simple. I have a secret Pinterest board titled "It's mine. It's out there. I deserve it." I post pictures there that evoke powerful feelings inside of me: Sailboats, cities, people, and nature. It's a collage that excites, and motivates me every time I open it. It's on my phone. It's in the background when I'm working on my computer, and it's on my huge desktop when I'm just chilling around the house. There's another secret board in my Pinterest. It's titled "Thank you for your wisdom." I post people, and messages there that give me strength, and direction.

By building these boards, I have in a sense created bumpers in the bowling alley of life. Isn't life just a game anyway? It is, but I prefer to see it as a golf game, "You against you." You might say, "mishit." I say "mis-thought." You may say, "yanked." I'd say, "off-center." The game of golf, and arguably all games are really about mastering your mind. Focusing on the subtleties...

So until we can all bowl solid strikes and hit shots down the middle every time, may we use visual aids to help draw in the focus, and stay out of the gutter. The gutter? Well, instead of scrolling Facebook too much, make sure to scroll your vision boards instead.
After all, like the little girl's t-shirt said, "don't wish for it, work for it." Work for love, work for freedom, work for a better world. As an old quote from the Dhammapada says "your work is to discover your work, and then with all your heart dedicate yourself to it."
We indeed magnify what we focus on. Why not program our subconscious on purpose rather than by default?

STITCH 024

Three Little Birds

"To affect the quality of the day, that is the highest of arts."

–Henry David Thoreau

I'd like to probe the symbolism of what a campfire is, why we build them, and what role they play in sustaining our well-being, today, and long term. Now, you might be wondering where this is going. I agree, it sounds out there.

Close your eyes, and imagine yourself at your favorite spot to build a fire.

Take a moment to think about the process of doing so, gathering sticks, acorns, logs, and the rest. Imagine you've managed to use your magic touch, and lighted the fire. Now sit back in your campfire posture, and let the dancing flames be a mantra for the following contemplation.

Every day you wake up, you are greeted with sensations: sounds, scents, light, dark, cold, warm, drive, will, desire, an array of other feelings, and a spectrum of life that is uniquely yours - as you have created it. Burning in your mind are remnants of a dream, perhaps a longing to hold on to the pillow and strive a moment longer for recollection until you decide it's time to get up. The house is as you've left it the night before, and soon the new day is taking shape. Perhaps you've looked at your phone, checked email, weather, the news? Suddenly, you're back on the digital plane.

Let's back up a second, and take a look at a different version of that sequence. What if instead of looking at your phone, you strapped on your sneakers, grabbed your iPod, and went outside. What would that feel like? Instead of bringing your phone, you grab your tunes, and head out the door. Your initial instinct is to check email, but then you realize it's just your iPod. You have no choice but to listen to music. Exiting your building/home, the physical world outside you is coming alive. The mood of the day is still all in your court, and whatever your jam is, is up to you. Run, walk, skip,

THE ARTISAN ENTREPRENEUR

find some swings... take your pick, because as far as you know, life is good, and you're just strolling with your rosy red glasses. Now, what's happening in the second sequence is simply a reorganizing of priorities. Instead of the waking world busting into your space, the waking you is busting into the world with the rhythm of your choosing. You're grounding, propelling through purpose, and expanding into flow: the WalknTalk mantra. Maybe even getting lost on an aimless morning jaunt.

Now about that campfire. In historical times, we couldn't just turn on lights, and start the electric stove. We had to build fires to stay warm, cook, and see. We had to tend to them before bed, and start them back up in the morning. Built into that required step of survival, building a fire, was a process. One that required our full, and undivided attention. If you look at the philosophy of Zen, that is the requirement; transcendence through oneness with body and mind. After all, the saying goes, 10% of life is what happens, and 90% is how we react to it. Imagine how great life would be if we reacted more often from our flow instead of its flow.

Okay, I confess, this morning I was a bit of an early bird, and felt like I got the worm. I woke up, quick made my bed as I do... put on my sneaks, grabbed my iPod, and ran down to the lake. I took a detour and ran in the grass. I remembered being a kid, playing soccer for a moment. I smelled the scent of grass, noticed beams of light hitting the trees from the sun, and then ran along the shoreline of the beach. It hit me that I often go to the beach but I never get that view. I ran a bit longer, took off my shoes and waded into the water. The cold was exhilarating. I did a few butterfly strokes and felt like flipper. The water was so clear that I could see the ripples in the sand. I waived to a friend passing along the beach. Before I knew it I was toweling off from my shower back inside and starting my day. I listened to Bob Marley, "Time will Tell, and Three little birds" on repeat the whole way. And wow, was my mug grinning. It made such a difference.

What I'm getting at here, is that the campfire we build is that gathering process that it takes to fully engage ourselves daily, morning and night, to really reap the benefits of living fully. There's a lot of talk these days about the power of habits. Rather than getting all gung-ho about habits, let's just get pumped about life wherever we are on its path. After all, as my Journalism professor paraphrasing Helen Keller said, "life is an adventure or it's nothing!"

STITCH 025

Go To The Gardens

"There are many good soldiers, few saints."

– Aldous Huxley

Have you ever considered the awesome power within you? The energizer bunny you can switch on if only you knew how to tap into your other self? Other self? You might be wondering what that is, and/ or where it might be found.

If so, great question.

In this moment, I'd like to dive into the success philosophy of Napoleon Hill only to identify a key to unlock an even more obscure author who holds a precious insight for us all to become the enlightened beings we are destined to be.

As a child, I would get off the bus, and walk up the driveway to my grandparents' house. Inside there was always an immense quiet coupled with the ticking of a sophisticated clock that sang with bells on the hour, half hour, and quarter 'til. I would set out my books to study, and Grandma would come to greet me with cookies and Pepsi; the elixir to life for any fifth grader. Shortly after, my grandfather would walk into the room, draw the curtains, and gazing out the window then return his gaze to a peculiar instrument hanging between the window panes. He would do this, and then say, "well, so long sonny."

One day I got up from my chair to inspect what he was always looking at. On the gauge read three words inside of an almost "speedometer like" circle. "Fair", "change," and "rain". I later learned that this instrument was called a barometer, and used to predict the weather.

Years ago I was walking in Prague with my music professor and spiritual guide, Igor. We were discussing our upcoming jaunt to the mountains to practice for our next concert, when I asked him about the weather. Igor stopped and placed one hand over my heart, and the other over my shoulder, saying; "Počasi je vždycky tady v uvnitř

THE ARTISAN ENTREPRENEUR

Nejte." This translates to "weather is always in here Nate." Igor was a source of tremendous growth, and inspiration for me at that time. And for many students for that matter.

To this day, I still think about what he said.

Not long ago, I was driving in my car and listening to the Napoleon Hill classic "Think and Grow Rich." In this book he talks about the steps one must take to achieve success. He says that at some point one almost always meets with temporary defeat. He says that it is during this time that one meets one's "other self."

The other self is the higher expressed, deeper purposed, more energized and committed version of "you" that will not give up. The one that emerges to meet the road wherever it may lie.

What he doesn't say is, how one locates the "barometer" to address the weather inside, and then even influence it in a way that is favorable to one's success? And beyond success, how does one redirect that weather to become enlightened and reflect that of peaceful gardens, perhaps like those of the Self Realization Fellowship center in Encinitas, California?
So glad you should ask.
An obscure philosopher named Aldous Huxley published a book in the mid-1940s that might have just what we are looking for. He is most famous for his line about the doors of perception in which he says that "when the doors of perception are cleansed everything will appear as it is, infinite." The key we are looking for however emerges from an older text called the Perennial Philosophy, a complex text that was once referred to by the New York Times as "The most needed book in the world..." It was from this book that this "needed" book's most needed insight jumped out at me this morning when I turned to read my darling an inspirational thought to start the day. It reads:

"The saint is the one that knows that every moment of our human life is a moment of crisis; for at every moment we are called upon to make an all-important decision - to choose between the way that leads to death and spiritual darkness and the way that leads light and life between interests exclusively temporal and the eternal order; between our personal will, or the will of some projection of our personality, and the will of God." –Aldous Huxley, Perennial Philosophy.

As if this text is not riveting enough, Huxley goes onto make an even more dramatic comparison to soldiers and one's calling to the spiritual context of life.

"In order to fit himself to deal with the emergencies of his way of life, the saint undertakes appropriate training of mind and body, just as the soldier does. But whereas the objectives of military training are limited and very simple, namely, to make men courageous, cool-headed and cooperatively efficient in the business of killing other men, with whom, personally, the have no quarrel, the objectives of spiritual training are much less narrowly specialized. Here the aim is primarily to bring human beings to a state in which, because there are no longer any God-eclipsing obstacles between themselves and Reality, they are able to be aware continuously of the divine Ground of their own and all other beings; secondarily as a means to this end, to meet all, even the most trivial circumstances of daily living without malice, greed, self-assertion or voluntary ignorance, but consistently with love and understanding. Because its objectives are not limited, because, for the lover of God, every moment is a moment of crisis, spiritual training is incomparably more difficult and searching than military training. There are many good soldiers, few saints."

– Aldous Huxley, Perennial Philosophy.

Could it be that all of life is really meant to be lived in crisis? Well, that would possibly depend on how "deep" you would like to live it or contemplate its constructs. Society trains us to see crisis in frivolous matters and their surface implications instead of seeing crisis in terms of a deeper context of where those frivolous matters could potentially be leading us.

Could it be that our greatest gift is the crisis we are currently facing, and what we can learn about ourselves in facing it? Or the one we are avoiding to admit? Let's do the world a favor and honor more crisis, and recognize that in choosing "light" we choose the sunny gardens of SRF in Encinitas, California, or wherever you envision your sunny gardens to be. May we recognize that those sunny open skies are just one deep breath away. One breath that, if concentrated, could vanquish the clouds of darkness hovering over our world today.

THE ARTISAN ENTREPRENEUR

Our destiny is found in leaning into our highest expression. Leaning into the breath.

STITCH 026

Paradigm Shift

"Once you have tasted flight, you will forever walk the earth with your eyes turned skyward, for there you have been, and there you will always long to return."

-Leonardo da Vinci

True or false, everything begins in the mind? True indeed. There is a phrase I live by that first found me as a child: "Be Bold and Mighty Forces WILL Come to you." This is from the movie Almost Famous, and originally written by Goethe.

Is it not the truth? That we step out and the net appears? For instance, I once needed a photographer for an important event last minute. I trusted that one would show up, and naturally I met a photographer willing to shoot the event a week prior. It happened naturally...

I'd like to focus on this: the act of committing to boldness; committing to the thought
/ inspiration that originally presents itself in the moment of "aha", and following it through to fruition. Why? We are all simply possible points of expression for the infinite wisdom, love, and creativity that exists within the world.

And all of that goodness seems to come in lightning bolt moments of "aha"... Fear I was talking with a friend today about using her image in her marketing with regard to her business. She said she was shy to do so, but knew she should. I asked her...

"Do you believe in what you do? Do you love what you do, and wish to make the world a better place through it?"

Naturally, she said yes.

THE ARTISAN ENTREPRENEUR

I continued. "Well then use your gift, your smile, and your uniqueness to communicate that desire with the simplest and most powerful expression of you... Yourself."

Can we wait?

If we all died tomorrow, we would regret not only what we did not do, but more deeply what we did not give. Not giving our "moments of aha" would be comparable to Motown records recording the hits of a century and keeping them all in the studio for fear that they would not fly.

Let it Go

May we remember always that ideas are born with wings, ready and willing to fly. It's our own fear that keeps them in the birdcage.

STITCH 027

The Greatest Great

"The flower that blooms in adversity is the rarest and most beautiful of all."

–Walt Disney

Have you ever wondered what makes "the greats" great? What gives them their edge? Perhaps you might be wondering where they even find the path to the greatness that comes from them, the one that sustains and continues long after they are gone. Is there actually such a formula that exists to create greatness?

I will be sharing a story that illuminates a new definition for what I believe is at the center of greatness: Inspiration.

In probing where the term "inspiration" comes from, and redefining what it is, my hope is that we may be left holding a new tool to keep us all on the course to harnessing more of our own greatness, everyday.

Years ago, I was looking up a skyscraper in downtown Chicago when something occurred to me. Almost all of these gorgeous feats of mankind seemed to be adorned by one common shape – a spire. I thought of my beloved city of Prague in Czech Republic and recalled its nickname, "the city of a thousand spires." Could it be that a spire is more than a decoration on top of a building? But rather a clue to how the building was created? What about the architects that built all of those buildings? Were they all thinking the same thing, or just using a common shape to finish off their masterpieces?

Traditionally inspiration has been defined as "in spirit". However, what if the definition of inspiration could be reduced to a shape, and explained through an untraditional method of etymology? I began thinking about the pursuit of an idea. The beginning, when it flashes in your mind, and then the feeling of commitment that occurs when you decide to make it happen.

THE ARTISAN ENTREPRENEUR

At first you become "inspired." You see the top of the structure, building, or idea you're looking to create. You feel the likeness of the accomplishment that is now becoming your quest. The moment of inspiration fades, and your gaze finds the horizon. You think to yourself...and then you choose...To aspire. You say, "I will aspire to achieve this vision."

The act of aspiring sends you into the mode of pursuit. Pursuit follows the path inward listening to intuition as it becomes your guiding force. Before you know it, many see you spinning, running, pursuing, and inexhaustibly committed to attaining what you originally saw, felt, and knew as true.

At this point, you are inside of your vision, taking the steps to make it real. You have been "inspired," and now through aspiring ... you take on the shape of "a spire."

You spin and step in the direction of pursuit, until it becomes obvious that your life is taking on a new a shape. It's the shape of inspiration. You are becoming a spire. Taking a step back into the original question of what makes the greats great, I'd say the answer has to do with a shape of their lives. If we look at our own lives, we might ask, where are we already "in spire," and where do we need to get clear and become more of "a spire".

The easiest way to do this is to resort to this mantra: "If our life is a book that we are writing, what do we want the main character, that is you or me, to do? What is the story that you ultimately want to tell?"

This Theory of Inspiration is something I have pondered for many years now. I pondered it so long that one day I decided to make a video about this theory.

You can find it at: www.inspirationtheory.xyz

STITCH 028

Déjá Vu

"The mind can never find the solution, nor can it afford to allow you to find the solution, because it is itself an intrinsic part of the 'problem.'"

–Eckhart Tolle

Have you ever had the feeling like life is repeating itself?

Like your daydreaming has become something that is overtaking your present moment more often than you'd care to admit? What would it be like to jump out of our heads, and live what we're thinking about? Wouldn't that be satisfying! Hmm, but how?

I would like to propose a simple solution. That solution comes through the wisdom of an old Czech music teacher and could quite possibly hold the key to making this year, this moment, and this chapter a downright success!

Are you ready?

It's simple but profound, and the only way to really get it is through the setting of a Czech pub.

Years ago, I was an exchange student in Prague, Czech Republic for one year. It was the catalyst for learning another language, and a cornerstone to my entire vision of living an international life. What was unique about that year, and about the life that I began crafting there, were the voices present among my friends.

Everyone had one common value; being unique. The longer your hair, the funkier your style, and the more you, you could be, was all the better. While most of my Czech pals would argue that I was the protégé of a dreaded chap two years my minor, none would deny that we were all protégés of one man, and one man only, Igor.

THE ARTISAN ENTREPRENEUR

Igor was the school music teacher, and majestic man that so many of us admired. He had the presence of a Lord of the Rings character and the energy of a supernova. This is the guy that would shake your hand with the force of Zeus and stare into your eyes while smiling ear to ear just before hugging you with vice-grip strength. Only to then pull back, grab you by the shoulders, and repeat the process again.

He is also the one that led us to dream up trips to Czech cottages in the countryside where we would go to rehearse and play music, make art, and be ourselves. In terms of school trips, we had it made; all due to our extraordinary chaperone.

It was a couple of years ago that I was back in Prague making my annual trip when we met with Igor. A close friend of mine and I sat down with him like the old days. All of us there crammed in a Czech pub on the Castle. Clouds of smoke surrounded us, as we put our glasses into the air. Peter and I looked at Igor, then clinking glasses, and breaking silence we laughed, and gazed into each other's eyes.

"Ted a šahani", řikal Igor.

"Now, and Touching,"

Igor said.

The literal translation is obviously lacking. Igor was known for his new year's themes. Not necessarily resolutions, but actions and ideas to ponder. What he meant was to be here in the now, and touch those around us. He was all about connection.

Based on the world we live in, looking at screens as much as we do, it's hard to deny that we need some grounding. A verbal hello is not often enough. We need to be embraced, hugged, and told that we're loved.

Now and touching.

Do it now, hug your friends, embrace the love, life, and people that are around you, and just maybe something unimaginable will take place.

STITCH 029

Hello!

"The only people for me are the mad ones, the ones who are mad to live, mad to talk, mad to be saved, desirous of everything at the same time, the ones who never yawn or say a commonplace thing, but burn, burn, burn like fabulous yellow roman candles exploding like spiders across the stars."

–Jack Kerouac

How many times have you been standing in the same room as someone else, exchanging glances, and not said hello? Or felt something in your gut, and sought out another's opinion only to be convinced of the opposite?

It has come to my attention that our dreams are like love.

They must be desired, courted, and seized. It is up to us to find them and choose them as the artist chooses the muse, unless of course they find and choose us.

Over the past decade, I have realized that every trip is a vehicle for personal growth and transformation exactly as the WalknTalk philosophy states. What I have also come to notice is the mystical way these trips occur and reveal another piece of the road that is nearly never found on the map. I've alluded to this in videos I have created in short clips. However, I have yet to reveal what it is that somehow gives the universe the power to give us what we are truly seeking. That is because there is no secret.

It is simply in the art of hello.

And where the conversation leads… well, that is an entirely different story.

As some may know, saying hello to a man on a train four years ago led to an opportunity to attend an exclusive conference in Palm Springs, California. While there, surrounded by billions of dollars disguised as ordinary faces, in the space the size of a large living room, I realized that every one of those people followed something small to create their massive success.

THE ARTISAN ENTREPRENEUR

 They had the wisdom to think beyond their imagination, and the discipline to work to create a fortune for others. Looking back over the past three years, I have traveled a combined 20,000 miles, at least, seeking out mentors and meeting people I had never met face to face but only through common friends and acquaintances just because I was following my gut instincts. The result has been a lot of magical moments, and unforgettable first in person impressions, eye to eye, revealing that my intuition has been right every step of the way.

While I can't responsibly sit here and tell anyone to habitually talk with strangers, I can say that I believe that whatever we lack, yearn for, or long to create in our life is out there, and seems to come find us when we're on the road.

STITCH 030

Slip Sliding Away

"But only in their dreams can men truly be free. It was always thus, and always thus will be."

-Dead Poets Society

Have you ever thought about what it means to ring in the new year? It occurred to me that if life were a song, December would be a moment of crescendo, that somehow dances off into the living room, and then dies into a white noise of familiar sounds and voices singing in our ears as we hopefully close our eyes for just a moment before it all slips away once more.

That's right, like the Paul Simon song; "slip sliding away... slip sliding away.... the nearer your destination, the more you're slip sliding away." Like finding the trap door in the library, we seem to have slipped into another chapter. This time, let's catch it before it runs away.

Catch it? Catch what? The year? No, not the year. The moment.

It's time to be on time. Timeliness is tough for me as well, but I mean being on time in a whole other sense. This isn't just a call to renew accountability on showing up on the dot, but rather having the presence to notice the dot, and draw with it. Abstract? Hm, perhaps a little... Okay, a lot.

Let's walk n talk.

When I mean catch it, I mean catch your tongue, catch your wandering mind, catch your yearning heart, catch your chance, catch life as it comes.

How? Well, let's start with an infinity pad... or a Tom Sawyer Journal. But no, actually it's the awareness that happens before the pen touches the paper that we're pointing toward here.

Let's go ahead and take a look at where our minds have wandered over the break. Truthfully we all know it's out there... that reality we would just love to live in. Many people of various kinds have famously said..."Life is about connecting the dots." But before we can connect them we must notice them in the first place. Is it not so?

If this is truly the New Year, then must we not ask what adventure awaits? Who are the people that are just dying to come into our lives? When is a better time to actually say, 'yes', this is the year?

The best time is now. The time is actually right now. Of course, if we wait, the time then will be now again, and then again why would we wait?

In the book the alchemist by Paulo Coelho, he talks about beginners' luck. He says that those who are just beginning are destined to have good luck. So if that's not reason enough to say yes this is the year to go get it, live it, and do it, then tell me what is.

Dreams: we want them and they want them. Our dreams want us. Like the song, "I want you to want me..."

But really, that's basically what our dreams are. They are dancing Romeo's and Juliet's in our minds saying, "I need you to need me." Okay enough, you get the picture. Our dreams want us as much as we want them. Without us, where does that leave them? We all yearn to be seen, right? Right. Well... so do our dreams.

I'd like to propose a quest, may this year be better because our awareness of these things is stronger, our willingness to give in to something less; weaker, and our determination to live fully, at an all-time high.

If you're still wondering how, do not worry... there is no right way. Perhaps we say it best with this simple phrase.

Live. Write. Now.

Let's go get those dots, color those moments, and pen this chapter with drive, love, and determination to live it like it's our last.

STITCH 031

Santa Is Real

"Anything the mind of man can conceive and believe, it can achieve."

–Napoleon Hill

Do you sometimes feel disconnected to the true meaning of the holidays? Like somehow you're just going through the motions? Well, today I would like to share a brief story that I found quite inspiring. And who knows, it may just put the spirit back in your eggnog.

I was sitting down to a warm fire over a drink with a friend in downtown Chicago this week. She said, "We told our son that Santa isn't real this week."

"Really?" I said.

"Yes, and no elf on the shelf either," she snickered.

I thought to myself "that's sad," then remembered when I found out. She then turned to me and said something so brilliant.

"Well, he learned to believe, didn't he?" she said, "Isn't that the whole point, anyway? To teach you to Believe in something you can't see..."

Believing isn't just a religious or a faith-based concept. From this I realized that it may be even simpler than that. Perhaps belief is the key to trusting the process of manifesting your next big breakthrough; a turning point that only a long tunnel of unknowns could create for you.

Belief + Trust + Time (to evolve your that trust) = Faith in motion -> a key mechanism for the process of manifesting anything (even your most desired holiday gift ;)

STITCH 032

Click Click

"The road to the City of Emeralds is paved with yellow brick."

–L. Frank Baum

Can you imagine a world where no one followed their dreams? A bleak, shadowy existence where everything remained sad, tattered, and broken? As I look at the steam rising from my coffee mug next to me, I smile and sigh, "impossible." According to the Desiderata, there is a perennial force of love that "permeates and penetrates every crevice of the universe," and that love is in us all.

I feel we must explore how we mask our light, our talents, and our potential with fear. This is a battle that we enter into at birth, and it is in this battle that we discover the sides of life that can take us into places beyond the borders of the "safety zone." That's right, it's in navigating by the light of the fireflies, the stars, and the moon, that we make it through the "scary forest." On the other side of fear is a beach, ocean, and a sailboat waiting for us to sail off into the sunset of transformation. Shall we?

Finishing a page-turning novel last week, the audio concluded, and I wondered what I should read or listen to next. Something told me to look up the Wizard of Oz. I joke that I never saw the Wizard of Oz as a child because I was busy swinging a hammer, and building tree forts.

"Whenever you are feeling drawn towards something, there is most certainly a clue waiting there for you" – The Celestine Prophecy

Or in some cases, like Dorothy, you are pulled, caught in a storm, and your life changes before your eyes. You long for something that you lost, and in the process of surviving the storm you are somehow "knighted, kinged, or queened with silver boots and a golden hat." Unbeknownst to you, your yearning becomes a force that leads you down a "yellow brick road," one that you must follow if you are to discover your greatness. It is in these moments that everything changes.

THE ARTISAN ENTREPRENEUR

I wonder how many children watching the Wizard of Oz remember how powerful Dorothy is with her silver boots, and that she is seen as powerful even to the wicked witch of the south, though she doesn't have the slightest clue that she is. Isn't it funny that some people can be afraid of our power, but then realize we are unaware of it, and do everything to keep us in the dark about it, as the wicked witch does? Perhaps tragic is the more accurate adjective. Fear only continues to exist because it is somehow perpetuated by darkness.

However, on the other side of fear is always a smiling face over-flowing with love and light. For instance, each one of the characters in the book finally get what they've been yearning for even though it was theirs all along. They begin lighting up with love and confidence as they all become heroes. The cowardly lion always had courage, the Tin Woodman always had heart, the Scarecrow always had brains, and Dorothy always had the power to go back to Kansas with two clicks of her heels, and three short steps, though she had no idea that was possible. Why? They had to discover these powers. They had to earn them. They had to spend time in uncertainty, pain, and fear in order to grow.

As preacher John Hannah of New Life Covenant Church would say, "they had to have process." Troubling isn't it, that they had to risk their lives to kill the wicked witch of the south and the west in order to be cured by a Wizard who confessed he didn't have magical powers at all? Hardly... It was in risking their lives together that they became brave, wise, and powerful.

Might there be a place of uncertainty in your life that you're currently traveling through? Might it be possible that this uncertainty could be avoided by taking an easier way out? Isn't it best to stay safe, and not take too many chances? Safe is best, isn't it? How often does entertaining an exciting thought ever equate to playing it safe? It doesn't. Playing it safe usually feels like drinking flat soda. There's not a whole lot of satisfaction or excitement in drinking it. Neither is there in playing it safe.

The human spirit yearns to grow, dream, and discover. It is this yearning that causes our growth, sets in motion our greatest adventures, and if we are lucky one day gives us a golden moment when we realize that what we have been searching for was right there with us all along. My ears perk up and my heart flutters as I am suddenly

STITCH

reminded of the Alchemist, and the wind's laughter when Santiago returns to the Chapel under the sycamore to dig up his treasure.

"You old sorcerer you knew the whole story, you even left a bit of gold at the monastery so I could get back to this church. The monk laughed when he saw me come back in tatters, couldn't you have at least saved me from that? "No ...." He heard the voice on the wind say. "If I had told you that, you wouldn't have seen the pyramids. They're beautiful aren't they?" – The Alchemist

Santiago would have never seen the pyramids had he not followed his recurring dream, and Dorothy would have stayed lost in the Emerald City, not to mention her good friends, had she shrunken in the face of her quest. Neither would have discovered their greatness, and neither would have become the legends that they are; not in the books, not in our hearts, and not in the awareness of the world. They are the fireflies in the forest, the stars in the sky, and the moon rising over our ship mooring there just off the beach on the other side of the brush. Could it be that we are closer to setting sail into our own transformation than we realize? If you need to wonder, perhaps take a moment to watch the colors changing in the sunset sky. There is only one way to find out.

STITCH 033

Dating Destiny

"Oh love is real enough; you will find it someday, but it has one archenemy—and that is life."

-Jean Anouilh Ardeler

How many of us have sat around wishing we were gearing up for a hot date? Perhaps perusing posh restaurants online waiting for the love of our lives to text us the time and place?

Good, now take a deep breath, relax, and let's ask ourselves a question. What if all the energy exhausted wishing for others to love us was poured into a process of loving ourselves that translated into more hot dates than Walt Disney himself could round up?

"I beg your pardon? Hot dates?"

"Well, dates with destiny of course."

That's right, I want to take a look together at a formula for getting those "hot dates," and ultimately courting the life we are truly longing to live; recognizing that courting that life begins with courting ourselves.

The tremendous spiritual teacher and author Wayne Dyer once said: "You cannot give away, what you do not already have." When you think about it, if "like attracts like" and "love attracts love" then wouldn't it make sense to put love into everything we do if we truly wanted to attract love into our lives?

Let's face it, being an adult is a challenge. There are pressures, stresses, and problems that come with being in charge. But what would life look like if we just stepped back, and lightened up a bit? Perhaps, let go of a few things that we've been carrying around, that honestly are weighing us down, and do not necessarily serve us at all.

If you'd like, take a moment to close your eyes and recognize what those weights might be. Good. Now, pretend they're rocks, and just toss them off to the side down by the seashore. How does that feel? Lighter, we hope. I can remember walking through Torres del Paine in Patagonia, on a four-day trekking trip listening to Wayne Dyer's disc titled There's a Spiritual Solution to every Problem.

I recall a story he told about his little daughter loving animals, and how each time they went to the forest, butterflies couldn't help but land on her. He had a brilliant explanation for why this is. He said, "all living creatures will cease to feel fear in the presence of those that can send love in response to hate" (quoting Patanjali).

If you think about it, aren't butterflies usually the symbol for transformation, once cocooned, and then suddenly free? Well, I think Dyer's story is telling us that the more peace we can feel, the more love we can have.

"Is love heavy or light?"
"Well, if it's like those butterflies, then it's light of course."

Many of the Buddhist philosophers claim that the path to enlightenment and happiness is really just a path toward letting go, one of emptying ourselves of those things that no longer serve us. I suppose we could say that would entail tossing a few more rocks into the sea and feeling more like the butterflies in the forest. Could falling in love be similar to the process of becoming enlightened? Well, most people usually think those falling in love are going crazy, but then seem to want what they have anyway, so perhaps it could.

What I'd like to know is what it's like when the butterfly goes from living in the cocoon, to flying around effortlessly. Perhaps if we took some time to imagine what the patience of that process would require, then maybe we too could sense the moment when it's finally time to break free and fly effortlessly.

The famous philosopher Henry David Thoreau once said that true wealth and happiness is defined by "the number of things one can afford to let alone." Perhaps

STITCH

courting the love of our lives could happen naturally as we learned to let go, have peace, and bravely break free from what does not serve us like the butterfly breaking free from the cocoon.

Wherever we are, whatever life we've created, perhaps today is a good day to look around, and find a little more peace with it all. Perhaps then, the butterflies will start swarming us with more love than we could ask for. Here's to courting love cordially inside, until love occurs naturally everywhere we go.

STITCH 034

Law Of Love

"I will reveal to you a love potion, without medicine, without herbs, without any witch's magic; if you want to be loved, then LOVE."

-HECATON OF RHODES

It is so important to shift love into every single nook and cranny of all that we do.

Have you ever considered the importance of love in your life? The power it can have to truly transform the way you walk through the world? The joy it can bring to every moment, and the peace it can increase in your heart?

Yes, the answer is yes; this all-encompassing sound that touches every particle of us that is seeking validation. Yes, to your dreams you are considering. Yes, they are real, and most importantly yes, to you. You matter.

Imagine you are sitting on a couch observing the moment, and a cat jumps up on your lap. You hear the deep purring sound it makes, and you watch its eyes twinkle as every muscle of the cat's body forces itself up against you seeking a loving caress. The cat's need for affection is infectious. You pet it, snuggle it, and intend to love it with all of the desire inside of you. Like a silk pillow, you clutch it, and press your cheek against it's loving body until you have the restrain to let it go. Eventually, the cat jumps from the couch and your gaze returns to the moment. You realize the cat somehow gave you something you were missing all along, that the level of love in your body was somehow heightened by this experience.

There was a moment in my life where I had the pleasure of feeling this increase. Not from a cat, but from a church. Last Thursday evening a friend of mine said, "Come to Church with me."
"On a Thursday night?" I exclaimed.

THE ARTISAN ENTREPRENEUR

"Yes, you'll love it, and it would mean so much to me," she insisted. She had just been to a Lisa Nichols conference in California, and felt the calling to assist other people in finding their path.

"Isn't that in a bad part of town?" I worried.

"Southside? Come on… it's church. It can't be that bad," she said. As we parked and walked in I could hear powerful music being performed all the way from the other side of the parking lot.

"This is going to be amazing," I told my friend giddily as we walked faster, almost skipping. The church doors were open, and gospel poured into our eardrums, swimming around and into our hearts until we both smiled and walked-in lighting up with every step we took forward. Could this really be church? I thought to myself. It felt like a paid concert, and I'd somehow gotten in for free. Loosening up, I began singing along, and just went with the flow. The pastor took the stage and teasing the congregation encouraged the love from our hearts to enter the space more and more. When everything finally calmed his sermon began.

He talked about process, and what it takes to follow a dream. He talked about being ready, willing, and able to step up to the plate at any given moment. Comparing the path we take to achieving our dreams to that of squeezing an olive.

"God's going to squeeze you" He said. "And that oil is precious" he continued. "It's with that oil that we can then open doors for others, but we ourselves first have to become clear about what that oil is. That there is a process required to get that oil, and it isn't all butterflies and rainbows."

The music began again and the whole congregation started singing, and praising God. I could have created any reason in the world why not to embrace all of this, but instead my heart opened, and I let go of any attachments and stigmas to titles and categories of worship. I prayed with the people and sang along. In that moment my heart opened, and an ecstasy filled my body. Overwhelmed with gratitude tears ran over my cheeks, and I said, "thank you. Thank you for this experience. Thank you for this journey, and thank you for these dreams."

STITCH

The gratitude I experienced in that moment opened me to see something new. At the end of the service my friend and I walked up to the pastor. He was wearing a strikingly similar pair of glasses as I was.

"Nice glasses" I said.

"Nice glasses, I was about to ask you about yours" he said. "Well thank you, I actually design them."

"Designed them!? Alright, now give me your card. Pastor Hannah's in trouble," he said. We giggled, and embraced. I thanked him for the tremendous service, and the opening I felt in my heart. There we were, giving the sign of peace to all as we walked out. I noticed a difference in the cadence of our step as we left the church, and walked back to the car.
That love that I felt, that was always there, somehow finally felt activated, switched on, and began pouring through me, almost as if an accuracy piece was updated in the timepiece in my heart. Instead of wondering what time it was, I just kept feeling every moment saying, "it's time...it's time..."

Whether or not we realize it, all of the dots are connecting everyday. Perhaps if we sharpen our instruments, trace those dots, and connect the lines, we'll see a tremendous constellation emerging. Like an oasis, and a waterfall of love flowing into it, into our lives; cleansing our thoughts, healing our hearts, and moving our spirits up, like octaves on an organ, to pump love into the nooks and crannies of our lives, and those of others. Our purpose is always all around us. And should we ever forget, just say "Here, kitty, kitty, kitty..."

STITCH 035

Pink Umbrella

"Go confidently in the direction of you dreams! Live the life you've imagined. As you simplify your life, the laws of the universe will be simpler."

–Henry David Thoreau

When I think of the roots of the life we are cultivating and the one that we truly wish to live, I can't help but prompt the question: what does that mean? Quite frankly, it's about friends and friendships. I'd like to share a quick snapshot from this past week, and hopefully offer a broader perspective into something I think we can all relate to; a longing to share and a deep need to discover life with others.

As I recall, it was a rainy hot summer day as I was getting off the train and began walking to a business event. The downpour had steadied to an even drizzle and tapered into an innocuous mist. I put away my umbrella and began strutting down the street. I started thinking about the flaneur... The French word for the walker, the individual walking for the sake of it, without a care of when she or he would stop, but just set on walking.

It was then that a pink umbrella appeared in front of me. Holding it, was an elegant gal full of life, color, and focus. The portrait of her crossing the street with her pink umbrella spoke to me. I snapped a picture and sped on. As I passed her, we exchanged glances and smiled. She commented on how I was dressed and I marveled at her pink umbrella. I confessed I took a picture of her crossing the street, and told what a great portrait she made. She smiled, and thanked me.

Spinning my umbrella handle, I walked on. Lost in a blissful summer moment, the muse had wandered from my headphones, into my camera, and back to the tunes I was stepping to. I could feel excitement building as I neared the venue. According to Google maps, I was just a few blocks away when I heard someone call my name. It was my buddy Jeff that asked, "Nathan, where are you going? The event is that way," as he gestured behind me, and pointed his arm through the car window. Had he not seen me, my route might have taken longer, and I probably wouldn't have minded.

But what occurred to me at that moment is what I think is worth putting down on paper. I opened my infinity pad and took a note. He got out of the car and said "come on." I told him I would be there in just a minute. Circles of people were moving about through the glass, and I was about to be one of them.

What occurred to me on that sidewalk is simple.

Here we are walking through life, taking in beauty, and observing the world around us. If we are lucky, we have a few friends to remind us where we are going. I took another look at my infinity pad and thought about the pink umbrella. I recalled the way it made me feel and the interesting distraction it presented. Could it be that all life is just a series of pink umbrellas, memories of misty afternoons, and a handful of good friends passing through?

On the other side of the glass, where the business event was being held, was a recently new reality waiting to unfold yet another unforgettable night. I didn't used to have so many unforgettable nights dressed in a suit in downtown Chicago, and in fact when the opportunity arose to join this organization holding these events, I saw it as an invitation. In my mind, the invitation had read, "join these people living life, and forge a new community of friends in this area. Build the niche you are longing to co- create in, and let it unfold with the flowing current of time."

The life I live now, and the one I was living one year ago are both beautiful, but they are not the same. The difference is in the vast amount of friends and friendships that have appeared by going "confidently in the direction of my dreams," and seeking to "live the life I have imagined," all while recognizing when to take the helm and make the tack (Thank you, Thoreau).

STITCH 036

Le Petit Prince

"Here is my secret. It is very simple: It is only with the heart that one can see rightly; what is essential is invisible to the eye."

–The Little Prince

This message is two-fold, and involves a small assignment that I think you will enjoy immensely.

This reflection below is about listening, not only to others, but to yourself – especially to yourself. When I think of this topic, I am reminded of a book titled The Power of Introverts in a World that Can't Stop Talking. A good one, but I digress.

The assignment is simple: watch the Little Prince and notice the symbolism. Try not to make judgments about the characters or yourself based on what you notice through watching these characters. Instead, notice the different perspectives of the roles in this film, and notice them as ways of being. Think, which role am I currently playing? Perhaps I am playing multiple roles: are these roles contradictory or complementary, and what will my life look like if I keep playing these roles as such?

Here's some food for thought.

The other day I was talking with a friend in passing. She asked if I had heard of the Little Prince and said there was a great film out about it on Netflix. Surely I had read the book, but I'd forgotten all together what it was about. My inner voice shouted at me, "Dreams! Hello... it's about following your dreams, and not forgetting who you are! Duh, right? Wrong... should be a duh, but it's not." I sat down early one morning all prepped and ready to tackle a mountain of work. I was nestled in a quiet library overlooking Lake Michigan with the whole day ahead of me. I noticed myself skipping around my computer and avoiding the main tasks on the calendar. After a while I decided it was time for a change of scenery. I broke for lunch, then swam in the lake for a while, and eventually plopped down on a comfy couch at a cafe near the house. I still felt totally lethargic, and just decided to surrender my efforts to summon the muse until later. Something told me to watch the Little Prince, so I did.

What stuck with me most was the moment when the little girl finds the prince sweeping chimneys. Somehow he had forgotten who he was, where he was from, and all about the stars! Impossible, right!? Wrong... Ask me what I had for dinner last Tuesday. I'm pretty sure I don't recall.

The fact of the matter is that we forget certain things, even moments of absolute joy and celebration. Sadly, they too become like artifacts in our past.

The question I pose to all of us is, what are we going to do about it? The cliché answer, which is also full of truth, might be to live like there is no tomorrow, and seize every moment. Well of course... but what else is possible? What formula can we adopt to live out the lives that we will truly be happy to have lived, not just proud of?

I will leave you with this question as I ponder it some more myself, I will say this though. I have a hunch that the answer to remembering who we are, where we are heading, and what we truly wish to build our lives into involves being visionaries in the truest sense. Setting aside time to dream and explore ourselves on deeper levels than we had ever imagined possible by employing a particular being of ourselves... a visionary.

STITCH 037

45 Days

"Life is an adventure or it is nothing."

–Helen Keller

Today I'd like to tell you a story that begins in Portugal. Last winter, 2015, I was freezing up in a Portuguese attic wrapping every article of clothing around myself that I could find, which wasn't much being that my suitcase was a guitar bag, and yes it also was housing a guitar... When you think of Portugal you probably think of warm temperatures, blue skies, and Port wine. That's about 90% true, all except for the fact that they have no heat, and winter there is damper than Chicago in Spring when Winter just won't quit. It's the place where you learn the definition of a "three dog night" (a night so cold that you need three dogs to keep you warm).

I was cold, and even having trouble thinking straight surviving through the reprieve of brief hot showers that were for some reason boiling hot without a way to adjust them. I was living in a house with a team of videographers that allowed me to rent their barely inhabitable attic, and happened to be helping me shoot and edit my inspirational travel videos. The house was so cool, and being in their company was the best, so I decided to just go with it.

One day when I was up in the attic jamming away on my guitar, a knock came to the door. It was Zé introducing me to a friend of his who was coming to live in Chicago. His name was Ricardo. Ricardo was scrappy, smiley, and built like a surfer. He happened to be a surf fanatic, and also ran a video company that was most famous in Portugal for their incredible coverage of surf competitions, and music festivals. He told me he was moving to Chicago, and that we should meet up.

Standing in the tiny doorway of the attic I beamed a smile back at him, and said "come anytime man."

Six months later I received a Facebook message, "Mannnnn, we are here !!!!"

THE ARTISAN ENTREPRENEUR

I was struggling to remember who it was as those days were all just a blur from a spell of damp cold dreary nights in arguably one of those most enchanted places on earth; being that J.K. Rowling apparently derived her inspiration from there for her Harry Potter novels.

After circling the Willis Tower trying to find each other, we met with a huge embrace. Ricardo had lost his ID on the train to Chicago, and said the conductor took it. As he recanted the events of the train, I thought someone was going to call security as he became just about the most hilarious angry Portuguese man on earth. Ricardo crashed at my place the next few days, and became an instant pal.

During the Fall of 2015 we bonded through business, cinematography, and a vision to shoot amazing videos together. In January of this year I wrote a voiceover for a video I wanted to shoot for our wooden bikes. We tried braving the cold, but time ran out, and Ricardo was heading back to Portugal for a visit. We decided to put the project off until we could shoot it right with green treetop coverage, and summer air to fill the screen. On short notice, Ricardo messaged me on a Saturday, and said he had a cancellation, asking if we could shoot this week instead of in July. I cleared my calendar.

On a Monday morning at 11:15 AM to 9:30 PM we raced around Chicago to capture one of the most breath-taking glimpses of the Chicago Skyline that I could have ever imagined, coupled with the wooden bicycle. We met with hurtles that included: lost equipment, rented equipment, downtown clothes shopping as Ricardo needed pants to enter upstairs in the Willis Tower, and of course carefully assembling and disassembling the wooden bike several times to fit it in and out of his car.

With a little luck we finished editing the masterpiece, and were very proud to present it.

To watch our view, go to: www.woodenbicycles.com

Reflections
In retrospect, not only did this video turn heads online, it was the main video that caught best selling author of Three Feet From Gold, Greg Reid's attention to invite me to his conference in Los Angeles a year later. This video gave him the confidence

STITCH

to believe in me, and won me a spot on his stage to talk about what I do in front of some of the most impressive people I've ever met. To top it all off, that video caught the eyes of my love, and partner in crime who I met at Greg Reid's conference, Secret Knock, that day in the audience. She and I have been on an incredible spiritual and entrepreneurial adventure ever since. And when the next dots are connected, this bike is going to be even more valuable!

This brings me to another thought. Often we are tinkering, "following the spirit" working on projects that many people don't understand. As visionaries and dreamers we are criticized for the ways these plans will "never work out," or how these products we create will "never sell". I find that the people closest to you, especially certain family members (not all) are the biggest "dream stealers" out there. There comes a time when you have to stop talking to them about your businesses, plans, and dreams. While I'm the biggest proponent of "singing the song of yourself" as Whitman would say, and speaking your way into your success, I am also now the honorary PHD holder of keeping my mouth shut around those that reliably and consistently whether consciously or unconsciously deflate my hopes and the hopes and dreams of others because of their lack of self awareness, or disempowering story that they are telling themselves.

Take for instance a paraphrased quote from Prentice Mulfort in his work, Thoughts Are Things in which he states that to steal someone's mental property is just as criminal as stealing their physical property. It is meant that to deflate another, discourage, or through passive aggression harm their dreams (mental state) through verbal abuse in any way is literally the same as damaging their physical property, and he goes on to say that it should also be considered punishable by law.

Now think of the great philosophers of history, most iconic Socrates, who was condemned to death for "refusing to recognize the gods recognized by the state" and of "corrupting the youth," and then made to drink the hemlock poison. Socrates challenged the state or the "state of us—status" quo. Dreams you have are also often threatening to others because people are afraid that you will become something greater than them. Instead of celebrating your success they take it personally, and whether consciously or subconsciously, they begin attempts to undermine and cripple your success.

THE ARTISAN ENTREPRENEUR

As Mother Theresa says "if you are successful you will win some unfaithful friends and some genuine enemies. SUCCEED ANYWAY," –Mother Theresa.
In closing, there is one last majorly important point to be made. Wallace Wattles, in his book the Science of Getting Rich, talks about the competitive mind versus the creative mind. He says that our most powerful wealth creation mindset comes from the creative mind, the one that is synthesizing not polarizing. The competitive mindset does little for oneself nor for others acting as if resources are limited. While he assures that wealth is often and can of course be created through the competitive mindset, it acts from a place of limitation instead of a place of abundance.

For instance, two people selling insurance might be selling the same product, and therefore seem to be in the competitive mind, however it is their approach that determines whether or not they are using the competitive mind or the creative mind. Our job is not to fault others or point fingers. As stewards of light, and dream weavers "our work is" in the words of Buddha, simply "to discover our work, and then with all of our heart give ourselves to it".

STITCH 038

Vanishing Points

"Life is long enough, and it's been given to us in generous measure for accomplishing the greatest things, if the whole of it is well invested."

–Seneca

Do you remember drawing buildings or maps in art class as a kid? Perhaps you recall using a separate piece of paper that lie beneath the paper you were drawing on? Did it have little dots in the corner off to the side helping to align your drawing?

You may not remember, but these little dots are called vanishing points that relate directly back to crafting the vision that we are all creating in our lives.

In life vanishing points often take the form of mentors. They are the voices in our heads, and the invisible council that only we, the architects, can see.

These vanishing points represent perspective, wisdom, direction, and the other ethereal stuff that is often intangible and difficult to define.

Years ago I'd heard about a professor at college that nearly made someone cry despite his very small stature. He walked up to the student, and in a very thick accent said, "who are you?" The student stared blankly, and the professor responded, "that's right, you don't even know". News spread around school of a wise professor in his seventies from Sri Lanka. I immediately began attending classes, and even though I wasn't required to be there, made sure I was present.

What followed was a tremendous semester that turned into a deep friendship, and an everlasting appreciation for Buddhist philosophy.

Fast forward to a Sunday morning sitting on the beach in Chicago, when I realized that I owed Dr. Wicks a phone call.

THE ARTISAN ENTREPRENEUR

It had been years since we'd been to coffee, and I was feeling like I needed to check in with him. It was only then that it dawned on me. Was Dr. Wicks even still alive? Had I taken for granted his mortality, overlooking the fact that he was already into his later years? I rang, and his wife answered. Summoning the courage to speak, I asked her if Dr. Wicks was in. She recognized my voice, and recalled me from years before. She said he had been suffering from Alzheimer's and Dementia. She spoke of how he loved his students, and would love to see me the following morning for coffee.

A few days later I stood before their door on the 32nd floor of a Chicago high-rise overlooking the lake crossing my fingers that I was doing the right thing. I took a deep breath, and knocked. A caretaker opened the door, and there behind him stood a frail old man. "Dr. Wicks!" I said. It was a magic moment. He held my hand for what felt like hours, smiling and gazing into my eyes. During my visit I told him and his wife about all of my projects, and adventures. He continuously interjected phrases in the Singhalese language, saying "who we are my friend... is always changing. Who are we?" I reminded him of the valuable phrases he had taught me years ago about being "kind to your mind," and recognizing that "everything in life is a process."

As I met his wife in person for the first time I told her the story Dr. Wicks had told us years ago about the first time he had met her. He was in the library walking with a stack of books when suddenly he saw the most beautiful girl, and dropped everything. He used to ask us the question "and who my friends is the boy writing the love letters and sending her flowers?"

What I think he wished to express to me yesterday is that sometimes you don't know why things happen as they do, including his ailment. As the door closed behind me, I realized he was my vanishing point. Witnessing a man I love and respect in a state of decline triggered a feeling of urgency in me. If that feeling could have been expressed it would have said:

"My friends please listen, for I feel we have forgotten! Life is a short trip, and I am afraid that the vision we are drawing must take into account the part of us that one day will not work the same as it always has. Draw with the perspective that one day it will not be you that is drawing the vision, but perhaps your legacy! Draw with every

STITCH

intuitive muscle in your body, take action, and do not delay – Tempus Fugit!" (Time flies).

STITCH 039

Keep The Hammer Down

"The successful person will profit from his mistakes and try again in a different way."

–Dale Carnegie

Have you ever wondered how to get "it" right the first time? Is that even possible? So many people have this vague sense that "life is about the journey". But what about when the journey involves risk, "opportunity cost", investment capital, etc? Isn't that adventure as well? Adventure with consequences! Like white water rafting, or climbing Everest, none return the same as when they left, and some not at all. Is the answer to "begin with the end in mind," as Stephen Covey advises? That makes sense, but how do you imagine the end? The end seems so unimaginable, and perhaps irrelevant. Is it not better to ask, "what is the story I would like to tell when all of this is over? Who did I decide to be when things got hard, and how did I perform when it really mattered?"

I would like to share a story about my most valuable production lesson that has been vital to WalknTalk's survival, and success. It might also give you an inside view into how I've developed a whole new brand, Big Murphy's, and what the learning curve taught me from the first time around.

The following story involves the designing and engineering of an iPhone case with the help of the Amish. (Go ahead laugh. Yes, even they have an iPhone, though they hardly turn it on).
Here we'll examine why you almost never get it right the first time around, and why and how you can go about turning the page, moving on, and "turning pro" as Steven Pressfield calls it in "The War of Art".

"Keep the hammer down, Nathan" -Marian, my Amish mentor.

THE ARTISAN ENTREPRENEUR

That is the voice I would hear almost every time I hung up the phone after tireless conversations. It was mid-September, 2012. Approaching our first four months of working together, the bond was real. I had only ever talked to them over the phone, and all correspondence, teaching my leather design and production to them, a process of trial and error, was done via thumbnail sketches, phone calls, and several back and forth trips to the post office. When we finally got the journals down pat, I had imagined creating an iPhone case. Marian and I thought they would be sure to sell. I spent hours, days, and weeks sitting at my workbench toiling away, like a caveman with an awl.

Creating iteration after iteration lead to a puzzling never-ending process. Two months went by before we finally decided that the design I'd made was something that they could produce.

Soon I realized that to "measure 100 times, build it once, and cut thousands of units" is the ideal process for building a product in leather. Unfortunately, reality often challenges mental theories when it comes to perfecting leather products.

After designing a product concept, step two to any leather design project is building a cutting die. Cutting dies are expensive, and once they're built in steel, there's not a whole lot you can do to change them. Similar to cutting leather, once it's cut, it's cut. If the die is wrong, so are your pieces, and so is your product. You might be catching on to where this story is heading.
Yes, expensive mistakes happen fast. And they happen even faster when you aren't there to notice them happening.

I got a phone call from the Amish.

"Uh, hello there, Mr. Nathan. Yeah, we got a problem here." I froze. "The hole for the phone camera was somehow built on the wrong side of the die."

"Are you kidding me!" I thought. I asked how many they had punched. It turned out they'd punched and branded seven hides worth of leather. That was about my entire stock for Christmas and I needed to profit to move ahead. I collapsed inside. I had been trying so hard to make this iPhone case, and somehow it was turning into a disaster. The cases arrived, all with the camera hole on the wrong side, branded, and along with them, an enormous bill for a product I couldn't sell.

There was no undoing what was done. I found ways to turn the strange pieces of leather into pouches I could sell and resolved to pull in the reins. Something needed to change about the way things were being done. So what did I do? I needed for this process of building the dies, cutting the initial pieces, and perfecting the first runs, to be something I could see and carry out in my studio.

My obstacle? Caveman tools. To make the process manageable, I would have to get the tools to do it. That meant getting a job and rolling up my sleeves. Slowly but surely I purchased machine after machine until I had built a mini product design laboratory. Years later, the cost of producing my leather dies has fallen ten times as I now source my dies from Eastern Europe and resell them. There's a neat video on there that shows you what a cutting die is, and how it's made. www. metalcuttingdies.com

In 2010 in Argentina, I sat down with my first rolls of leather, and imagined something like a metal stencil existing somewhere. I didn't know what a metal cutting die was, nor did I have any idea how much one should cost or about how to have one made. Looking back, that mistake has saved me more time and money than I care to imagine.

In fact, if I hadn't made that mistake early on, I would have never made it to this stage of the game. More growth has come from learning the process of die building, punching, and stamping than anything else. It's the meat and potatoes behind WalknTalk, and the reason why we can engineer products in-house so efficiently.

Now, back to getting it "right" the first time. Is it really about getting it right the first time, or is it about getting it right, period.

"Make a decision. Then make it work." – a family adage

When I look back at the iPhone case lesson, or the time when I was beside myself needing to redesign the Tom Sawyer journal, I realize how important it was to go through those stages.

THE ARTISAN ENTREPRENEUR

Now, how do these lessons play into building a new brand, and forming a new venture? Great question. It comes down to knowing that there will be things that go wrong. Absolutely. But how can we focus on the most important details, and at the end of the day not get stuck in maybe land? Branding is about taking a direction and sticking to it. Then down the road being humble enough to adapt and grow according to the feedback of others, and consumer demand. Stephen Pressfield in "The War of Art" talks about the force of resistance; procrastination. He even goes to the extent of saying that his first novel ruined the first decade of his adult life as he continued to put off writing it. His recommendation? Write, put it out there. Stop caring what other people think and take action. Without the action and the follow through, you're like a golfer standing up to hit the ball forgetting the importance of swinging!

I've recently adapted this mentality to writing. For my work, I realized that not every Tuesday is going to be the easiest to sit down and produce genuine content. But the act of writing without judging, doing my best, is what keeps me publishing. This concept of resistance is seen in the e-myth as well, in which they explore why most people that start businesses are not entrepreneurs but technicians who become entrepreneurs for a brief period, and then revert to being the technician, like me, residing over the workbench designing another new product when the others were already viable. Not to discount the value of doing so, but merely to highlight, that the growth comes in learning how to sit down intentionally, design, build, produce, and then shift back into the doing.

"Circulate to percolate" – My Dad

It's important to get out there, share your story, and learn about the journeys of others as well. I would attribute more to many of you reading this as my greatest help along the way than to anything else. Without a group of people who know you, your product, and your vision, it's hard to find traction. I've also noticed that they tend to be the first ones to know about your new brilliant ideas, and the best to keep you true to those ideas when doubts creep in.

Lastly, let's think. Is perfection ever something that can be expected off the bat? Not really. The solution? Putting into place habits of following through like a good golfer

STITCH

who knows the importance of holding his finish in the event that he stripes it down the middle when least expected.

After all, even a rusty stick has the potential of hitting a good miss or catching a member's bounce.

STITCH 040

Go Legend

"Fortune sides with the one who dares..."

–Virgil

Do you remember when you first saw the movie The Sandlot? When Benny was sitting in his room wondering what to do about getting that ball back from the 'giant gorilla dog'? Have you ever felt like Benny? Like maybe the peace in your life existed once you held that ball in your hands, and overcame the odds?

This prompts the question: "how do we make sure we become legends 'that never die, and not just heroes 'that get remembered'?"

According to the Babe, we only get one shot, and while it may seem easy to say "we'll do it." Actually putting on the PF Flyers, and jumping over the fence to face the beast is a whole other story.

Ready to go legend?

There is a friend of mine who flies planes. He also owns a company that at one point was building eighty stores a year for the Gap clothing company. You might think he's successful, and by every definition of the word, he is. However, if I told you he was a high school dropout, you might say, "wow, how'd he do it?"

The short answer is, "He dared," "He went legend," "He went all in."
A few days ago the two of us were talking on the phone about a big purchase I just made. I had told him how I'm at a big turning point in my life, and feel like a skydiver jumping out of a plane as I switch gears in some of my professional endeavors.

"Fuck it, try it on man. See how it fits," he said with a big smile.
There was a freedom in his voice. I recognized that as I already knew that I'd made the right decision, that the consideration of what others thought had been slowing me

down; like a ship tacking hard cutting through the water only to let up on the sheet instead of trimming the sail, and embracing the gust.

"Step into it Nathan," he said.
In that moment I thought about the Babe. The "sultan of swat, the king of clash, the legend." My mind wandered for a moment and a phrase entered into my head...

"If you think you can, or you think you can't, either way you'll be right."

-Unknown
I thought about the Babe, and every other legendary athlete. It was their "swag," their confidence, and their conviction that hit the home runs, not their bats.

In The Sandlot, Benny springs up from his bedside when his closet opens. The babe is there shouldering a bat, and puffing on a cigar.

"Don't go peeing your pants kid, I'm just here to help," he says.

Benny is in disbelief, struggling to believe the Babe is real.

"But you're..." Benny begins.
"Dead?" said the Babe. "Legends never die, kid."

Benny and the Babe go on for a bit about the pickle Benny's gotten himself into. The Babe quickly gets down to business.

"Let me tell you something kid, everyone gets one chance to do something great. Most people never take the chance either because they're too scared, or they don't recognize it when it spits on their shoes... This is your big chance, and you shouldn't let it go by. I mean do you remember when you busted the guts out of the ball the other day? Someone's telling you something kid, and if I was you, I would listen."

The Babe nonchalantly vanishes back into the closet, and Benny lingers contemplating by his bedside. A voice comes through the closet and says: "Remember kid, there's heroes and there's legends...heroes get remembered, but legends never die."

STITCH

You might be wondering where in your life that you're being a hero and not stepping up to own your legend.

If you're wondering what's holding you back, just think about the decisions you make, and ask yourself who you're making them for.

"Life is a puzzle. Every day there are new pieces swirling in our minds, it's up to us to put it together."
- Jeff Hoffman, Founder of Priceline.com

From what I can gather about all of this, intuition tells me that legends find the courage to claim their puzzle pieces, and then in countdown against the clock moments, go all in, and find a way to make it happen.

After all, if "fortune sides with the one who dares", what does it is grant the one who doesn't, but a lifetime of regret?

So my friends, wherever you are, whatever you're facing, strap on your PF Flyers, step up to the plate, and swing for the fences.

Go legend.

STITCH 041

Temptation Before Greatness

"I started my life with a single absolute: that the world was mine to shape in the image of my highest values and never to be given up to a lesser standard, no matter how long or hard the struggle."

–Ayn Rand, Atlas Shrugged

Is it true that "failing to plan is planning to fail?" It was said that Frank Lloyd Wright drew his best plan one hour before the client's arrival, and he was an enormous success. But what if you are the queen or king of the last minute? Someone that utterly triumphs over every deadline, performs at their best under pressure, and succeeds every time in the face of all odds? Well, good point. But succeed at what cost? While the argument can be made for the success of such practices, there is another side of the coin.

Have you ever felt like you were carrying the weight of the world on your shoulders, and didn't realize it until it bore down on top of you? Have you ever sadly or strangely found yourself somehow pinned down by illness, or distraught by not meeting your schedule?

There is challenging but benevolent territory to be found as we delve into the beauty of limits. Knowing them, and from there firmly standing on a foundation of self- knowledge, continue the climb. It is said that whenever there is something of looming importance we either get it done early, or wait until the last minute. While we tend to overestimate ourselves, we forget there is something more "rigid" than our own rogue tenacity, and that is "time". It is time with relation to health that either strikes a balance, or creates a disease. Could there be a better, or simpler way to understanding how to prioritize our lives? A principle that could act as a powerful decision making tool to help us choose more definitely when faced with a tempting commitment?

"Saying no to one thing means saying yes to another"

-Craig Collins, Creator of the Universal Reading Method.

Preparing for a very important event, I found myself saying yes to many other things, almost as a form of subconscious procrastination, and ultimately self-defeat. It wasn't until I was in the crucial window of getting everything done on time, that one extra commitment landed me in bed for twenty-four hours.

That's right, being the "yes" granted me a major "no."

No energy, no appetite, and no excuses. I laid there trying to stand up, and do work but I couldn't. There was some sort of virus that had infected my system.

"Do you know what animals do when they don't feel well, Nate?" Said Hans, my coach, good friend, and consultant at Ontoco.com.

"They lay down?" I said.

"That's right" Said Hans. "And do you know when they get back up?" he said. "When they feel better?"

"Ah, exactly..." He replied. My adrenalin kept kicking in as I said decidedly, "I have to keep going, this is just too important."

"Why didn't you do it sooner then?" I thought to myself.

"Hmm, well, there's no time for regretful questions like that now is there? Everything happens for a reason, and perhaps, it was time to merely embrace the pain of the lesson at hand."

I thought of Napoleon Hill and a quote I once read as I laid there struggling to even use a utensil to eat the rice at my bedside.

"With every failure comes the seed of equal, or greater success" -Napoleon Hill

STITCH

Time bore on, and finally I decided it was time to take Hans's advice, and just sleep. Before closing my eyes, I thought of my mentor awaiting these journals in California for this huge conference ranked number one on Inc Magazine's conferences of the year list. His name is Greg Reid, the author of Stickability, and he says, "When shit happens, use it as fertilizer."

The next morning came, and I was somehow cured of whatever was ailing me. Utterly grateful for the strength to get back to work, and continue moving towards my objective, I vowed to capitalize on the lesson. I had been listening to The Fountainhead by Ayn Rand the day before, and thought I would check out Atlas Shrugged. Often curious as to the meaning of the book's peculiar title, I found it on tape, and continued pouring over my work. In a moment, I stood up to tend to a whistling teakettle on the stove. I glanced out the window in eager excitement of the adventure that lay ahead the following day as I would soon be crossing the Rockies into California with a wish to make this trip a brilliant success.

At that second, the audiobook was describing the large Greek god, Atlas, holding the earth on his shoulders. What followed fit my current sentiment. I breathed, sipped and shrugged... The narrating voice said: "'If you saw Atlas, the giant who holds the world on his shoulders, if you saw that he stood, blood running down his chest, his knees buckling, his arms trembling but still trying to hold the world aloft with the last of his strength, and the greater his effort the heavier the world bore down upon his shoulders - What would you tell him?' 'I…don't know. What…could he do? What would you tell him?' 'To shrug.'"

While "shrugging" here may seem quite dramatic, perhaps it can mean telling ourselves a different story about our current circumstances? Letting the weight we're giving to one thing become more balanced as we gather perspective on the other. Ah, life is but a dream – a delicate one. Perhaps if we can become hyper aware of our limits, we can consciously outwit them by working less and relaxing more. After all, Tom Sawyer would approve.

STITCH 042

Burn The Ships

"Knowing others is wisdom; knowing the self is enlightenment. Mastering others requires force; mastering the self needs strength."

–Lao Tsu, Tao Te Ching, 33.

How many of us are convinced that we have something absolutely brilliant to share with the world, and that the hands of time have been tying us up for too long? That we are just done, fed up, and disgusted. That for too long our best has been withheld, and our magical gifts kept behind closed doors like Eucharist in the tabernacle?

There is a fascinating yet frustrating side of procrastination that needs to be explored. Why is it that the simple things that could bring us the greatest joy are the ones we put off doing the most? And why is it that we link pleasure to opening the refrigerator instead of typing the novel that could/would/will inspire millions to take action in their own lives? Are we not fulfilled more by giving than receiving? Inspiring, more than by being inspired? Is there any logic to why we go on putting off the actualization of our highest desires instead of facing them with full force?

On New Years Eve, my partner and I arrived to Chicago after driving back through a blizzard from New York. White-knuckling it through slushy roads and whiteouts at twenty miles per hour, I kept hearing a voice call to me. "Tell your story..." it said.

"I'm going to turn the closet into my office." I said. "The Metropolitan club is great, but there's too many distractions, and the work I'm being called to do this year is going to require a higher level of focus."

Arriving home, we prepared to greet the New Year with a new focus. I stripped the closet of all the clothes, and carefully examined the skeletal structure so unique to the space I had once sculpted to look like the bow cabin of a sailboat with a bunk and desk perched in the corner. While currently the closet had been housing my "tools"

THE ARTISAN ENTREPRENEUR

inside of a filing cabinet now half full of clothes, documents, and carpentry tools, my "design brain" revved with excitement to take the next steps.

In the corner of the closet I found three oars from my rowboat. I looked at them, and then carefully examined the ceiling underneath my loft.

"Why don't I just build a closet here in the living room, and hang our clothes from these oars?"

"Huh?" she said. Staring straight ahead, mentally building the oars into the loft, I nodded, proceeding without much verbal communication. I had slipped into that "zone" I spent roughly two years inside of while building the studio apartment into a quasi-eight-room-boathouse years before. It felt like drinking glacial water I hadn't tasted for years since the last great expedition; building.

I mounted the oars, rehung the clothes, and rearranged the closet. Books now lived on the shelf that once housed my toolbox, and a sliding glass cabinet now sat nestled in the space where clothing once hung. Inside stood ten sets of promotional cards, from my various current endeavors including a couple of my very first WalknTalk journals I'd ever made.

I continued decorating the space with all of the love, energy, and nourishment I knew I would need to create at the next level. And just to top it off, I reallocated my grandfather's stereo cassette deck, and turntable on top of the sliding glass cabinet. This year I decided to finally listen to all of these motivational cassettes my friend and owner of the Armadillo's Pillow, a famous used bookstore in Chicago, had gifted me. There are examples of writers who spent the majority of their time locking themselves in the bathroom to write, and plenty more I can't name doing other strange things.

But are such activities really so strange?

If we were to think about it, do you think more brilliant ideas have been harvested in large spaces or small spaces? With many people, or few people? With closed minds or open minds? What will we do differently this year to dislodge the pit of brilliance in our being, to release it with intention out into the world, and to raise a toast to others to support them to do the same? Is it any surprise that knowing someone who has done something you're trying to do makes it easier? That seeing it happen for them,

STITCH

demystifies the process for you? What proof are you looking for, do you need, to know that it is possible for you as well?

According to Martha Washington, "the greater part of our happiness or misery depends on our dispositions and not on our circumstances. We carry the seeds of the one or the other about with us in our minds wherever we go." Yesterday we spent the evening at the gym, and in the sauna. While many people lifted weights, sped along on treadmills, and climbed their way into the sky, I laid down quietly on a yoga mat.

Shakti Gawain, in Creative Visualization, talks about spending time in contemplation. If it's true that all of life first begins in the mind, would it not make sense to become masterful with our thoughts, to be impeccable with our motions, and meditative with our intentions? Is it not probable that in learning to move from this place, that we can begin to mobilize our highest desires with immense ease?

When we learn to exist from this place, nothing will seem hard, impossible, or unreasonable. Perhaps for this reason, we have the desire to undertake and achieve insurmountable feats... To bring us into a state of, well, enlightenment.

What space are you ready to create to manifest your brilliance? And what will it take to keep you there long enough to birth whatever contribution you are ready to make?

STITCH 043

Manifest Destiny

"Get Lost To Find Yourself."

–WalknTalk

Have you ever wondered how many days it takes to truly live a brilliant life? Or how to create the metrics with which to at some point deep down feel satisfied before you give your last breath to the material world?

Let's reconnect to the values that are shaping our lives. The one's creating our yes's and no's, the signposts on the trail of life.

Two years ago two friends sent me a message that they were both coming to stay with me in my four-hundred-and-fifty square foot apartment that I had built like a boat on the north side of Chicago. They were from the Czech Republic and had purchased two round trip tickets for a whopping five hundred dollars. When they told me they had intended to stay for three months, I nearly lost my mind.

I smiled through the Skype window, somewhat forcing my half excited grins until I realized the golden opportunity staring me straight in the face. They both lived in a beautiful apartment in Prague, and insisted that we simply swap for a portion of the time. I saw the writing on the wall, and quickly found my own five-hundred-dollar airfare through Istanbul for one of those painful eighteen-hour layovers that I secretly loved so much.

Before leaving Chicago, and giving my friends a thorough tour of the city including a glimpse into the networking life of an entrepreneur, we attended events in the Sears Tower, John Hancock Tower, and a steakhouse nestled in the Gold Coast. We softened every room we walked into. He with his red bowtie, she with her European wool coat, and me with my circular red-rimmed glasses I wore at the time.

As usual, departing for Czech was not easy. We ordered new hard drives, and other critical items to save my failing iMac that Marek was committed to fixing for me. I

THE ARTISAN ENTREPRENEUR

stuffed my luggage full of leather tools, journals, wallets, and other WalknTalk products. Literally leaving home with about ten minutes of flexibility, and praying I'd make it with my eyes closed and right arm wrapped tightly around the passenger seat headrest observing every move the UBER driving was making, convinced that my intent and urgency would increase his speed and skills for getting me there on time.

To think that this was a trip that just emerged somehow out of the ether, that in a parallel universe, they didn't buy the tickets and decide to come was a question that baffled me, still. And yet, I was on a mission to visit a few factories I had begun conversations with over the course of the previous few years.

This trip would stand to become the most fruitful, and one of the most life-changing entrepreneurial jaunts I was yet to make. Successfully bringing one hundred and fifty journals into a couple of shops in Portugal, finishing the design of my custom line of handmade eyewear, and creating a new brand called Big Murphy's originally with leather bags and belts, only to then become my latest success to date expanding into custom suits.

I was, needless to say, through this trip, transformed.

Is it safe to say that life does not give warning when it's about to all change in an instant? When things that you're pondering somehow become manifested ten times faster than you could have ever imagined?

A month after I returned, I was celebrating a subtle reunion with some business friends, and fellow entrepreneurs in the Sears Tower at a wine tasting. As a member of the club, everything was basically free, and of course the invitation was to indulge. Sitting down with a very close pal of mine, and reminiscing on the successes of the early 2016, we soaked in the moment with red tannins elevating our awareness levels to true bliss.

We were sitting in the Metropolitan Club on the 67th floor of the Sears Tower in the company of friends that we loved dearly, when our close friend seemed to be dozing off more than usual. We woke him, and all said our goodbyes that evening, as it was getting late.

Two days later I received an urgent phone call, then a text. "Our friend Art spent his last night on planet earth with us."

STITCH

I didn't quite understand. How? No one was over sixty years old among us. How could this be? I looked up at the ceiling above my lofted bed, and read a poem I had been once given by a banker. It read:

"Some day it will all come to an end. There will be no more minutes, hours, or days. It will not matter what you owned or what you are owed. It does not matter where you came from or where you ended up. What will matter is not what you bought, but what you have built. Not what you got, but what you gave. Not what you learned, but what you taught. Not your success, but your significance. Not your competence, but your character. What will matter is how long you will be remembered, by whom and for what. Living a life that matters does not happen by accident. You have to pay attention. It is not a matter of circumstance, but choice. Choose to live a life that matters. Pay attention to what matters most" -Michael Weber

I stumbled out of bed, placed a clean paper on the typewriter track, and wrote a song in his memory. I later performed it in his piano bar in downtown Chicago in front of fifty of his good friends and a business association that he gave his life to. When it was all said and done, he didn't need to live a day past fifty. He was a king in his own right, and soon crowned with an honorary street named after him outside of his famous bar.

My loft creaked as I clutched the pillow one morning and my love called out to me from the same table I had once sat at to write the song for Art. She was now sitting there writing her own tales about being a journalist in Syria, and the death tolls too high to count at present day that while she was there had reflected only a mere fraction.

She called out to me reflecting on the fragility of life, the rage of genocide, and the uncanny ways with which it all occurs. Whose call are you avoiding or embracing? What product are your developing or letting go of? What trip are you planning or taking?

May we always choose to make life the daring adventure that it must be.

There is only one way to find out if our dreams are real. And that is to make them real by acting in spite of them not despite of their existence. By noticing others, not ignoring them. By telling their stories, not forgetting them. And lastly, by telling our stories, celebrating our triumphs, and in doing so, inspire others to do so as well. With a humble breast, I bow. Thank you for choosing to live a life that matters by paying attention to what matters most. Journey on, and as always, thank you for listening. Not to me, but to your heart. Stitch your dreams. Sew your canvas. Paint again, no matter what.

STITCH 044

El Milagro

"Don't Quit Five Minutes Before The Miracle Happens."

– Dr. Greg S. Reid

Can you imagine a world whose existence literally depended upon the idea you were working day and night to create? A world that you magically saw unfurling before you like a gorgeous spinnaker slipping out of the bag from the deckhand below seamlessly coordinating with you as you concentrated on every last telltale gracing the mast as you painstakingly planned your tack with each and every intuitive molecule in every stitch and fiber of the fiberglass haul of the boat and body of you, your dream, and the reality both were so delicately tied to.

Two years ago I was dripping with sweat each day walking miles around downtown Chicago. From meeting to meeting, one to one networking, to peer to peer referral groups, to after hours business networking events, to committee meetings in the Metropolitan Club, River North Business Association, and BNI chapters around the city (Business Networking International). I recall my heels becoming blistered from all of the hoofing carrying samples, notebooks, dreams, sketches of products, and a laptop that together weighed enough to count as a metaphorical weight jacket trainers would use for bodybuilding. Instead of weight training, it felt like "wait" training, as in "how long could I wait/endure the financial, physical, and emotional duress it was taking to bring yet another brand/message/dream to life. To be honest, I loved it.
And even on the weekends when life really got hard slinging pizzas in one of the busiest restaurants in downtown Chicago, I did so effortlessly knowing one day it would all naturally fall into place.

I was training to have faith and keep to the path when all vital signs said pull back; I trudged on. Wondering if it was a sign I should slow down when one morning I woke up and couldn't put my shoes on. I found a pair of dressy sandals with an open back, and kept going.

Three years prior I had woken up from a dream in Prague after a great night. I had a dream to make leather bags. I was determined to do so, and like all good things that take time, I was prepared to wait for it. A friend lead me to a factory in the countryside, and a partnership was formed. A few years later the vision for the bags was born. It percolated. Sifting through family photos I found a story about my great grandfather, Big Murphy. He was known for "doing things with the wave of a friendly hand instead of the gesture with the sword," for being "large physically and mentally and doing everything in a big way." That's what I had surmised, and in fact usurped from an article I found written about him in the 1930's in a New York newspaper.

Truth be told my grandmother and I sat on the beach in Jupiter, Florida ten years prior while I conducted an oral history about her for a journalism class I was taking at Loyola University Chicago.

To my surprise Big Murphy was a defense attorney for bootleggers in the 1920s and 1930s, and my grandmother recalled slot machines disguised as flour bins in her basement growing up.
Tears came to her eyes as she recited a poem, written by Big Murphy's secretary's aunt who was a nun about Big Murphy's love for his mother, spoken at his funeral when he died at the age of 44. My grandmother was only 9 years old when it happened.

"Wilt thou a message take, for one who walks the golden way, she is my own, my very own, without her all are empty day. Whisper that my heart is with her. In that kingdom up above tell her that I miss her and I send her all my love. Dear God you will know my mother by the beauty of her smile. Wilt thou say to her, I'm coming home in just a little while."

And like that, she recited the entire poem, line for line without having heard, nor read it in over seventy years. Tears came to her eyes and mine. The personality of Big Murphy was something the world then wept terribly to lose. It was that magnetic charm, heart, and charisma that I was determined to bring back to life.

STITCH

"I'm having a launch for the new brand in November," I would say.

Whether engaging guests, colleagues, fellow entrepreneurs, or business club members around the city of Chicago, it seemed like that was all I could imagine focusing on. Every conversation ended with an invitation to the big bash that was imminent yet still without a launch date.

Meanwhile, I was working forty hour weekends at a famous pizza restaurant in downtown Chicago, foregoing sleep to build the dream. I had a crop of leather bags to pay for, a party to throw, and several new products in the pipe to roll out.

November drew closer and so did my golden birthday. I was turning 28 on the 28th of October, and my mother wanted to throw a big party for me in Rochester. While usually not fond of my own birthday parties, I agreed, and flew home.

Arriving home to Rochester, New York I was determined to find more records about Big Murphy's court cases, and stories about his life. A man in a cafe commented on my suit. He happened to be an archivist in the Rochester Public Library.

After following his directions, I found myself thumbing through the archaic archival system of the Rochester Public Library looking up information about the Charles W. Murphy, Big Murphy.

Pulling up several articles and a death certificate I took a closer look, and couldn't believe what I was seeing, or could I?

It was the date of his death that had my skin covered in goose bumps. I flashed back to a reading I had with an astrologer around the time I had created the brand six months earlier in the Spring. I wondered if I was crazy creating another brand while WalknTalk, my original brand was still working hard to become my main income, however I knew I had to do it.

Since I was a kid, forty-four was a number I had always seen in those synchronistic moments when I looked at a clock, cab, street sign, or plane ticket. Something told me Big Murphy was ready to come back to life, and I was ready to take the ride to make it happen.

THE ARTISAN ENTREPRENEUR

During those hot summer days pounding the pavement I had made arrangements with a bar in River North to host the launch party, but the bags weren't going to be done in time for the launch. I pushed the date, and on the recommendation of my trusted mentor Marty, I consulted with the Metropolitan Club about throwing the party 67 stories up in the sky.

The Sears Tower seemed like the most natural place to launch a brand like Big Murphy's, and while almost unfathomable that I would afford it at the time, they made me an offer I couldn't refuse and the stars aligned.

Aligned might be an understatement as the date they had offered, two days before Thanksgiving, was none other than the same date staring me in the face as I held the death certificate in my hand. November 22nd, 1938. Coincidentally this was the same day that the great JFK was assassinated, and the same date of the launch party. (To run the risk of sounding even more superstitious, he graduated from Syracuse Law in 1916, and I was using an iconic photo from his graduating class I found in some old boxes in my grandmothers basement to promote the brand. 1916 also happened to be year of the Easter Rising in Ireland when according to Wikipedia the "Irish end(ed) British rule in Ireland and establish(ed) an independent Irish Republic," obviously an iconic year symbolizing the re-establishment of values of freedom and autonomy for all who embrace the spirit of the Irish). If you're enjoying the coincidence, 22 is half of 44. I put two and two together, and found yet again the symbol that continuously kept leading me toward my dreams coming to fruition.

The night of the party came, and despite the Thanksgiving travel plans of so many Chicagoans, we graciously welcomed one hundred and fifty guests to the 66th and 67th floor of the Sears Tower in The Metropolitan Club for one of the most unforgettable nights of my life.

In all corners of the room were propped Big Murphy's posters mounted on foam core. Below each image boldly stood the statement "Make No Small Plans." The visionary who single-handedly envisioned the plan of the city of Chicago whose tenacity we all owe a unanimous bow of gratitude to is Daniel Burnham. He said "make no small plans for they have no magic to stir one's blood."

STITCH

The night shut with watery eyes from camera flashes, tears and laughs with friends, and the embrace of my graphic designer, a guy I had originally met at the 7 Eleven under my apartment six years prior. The same guy who believed in my vision, and stayed up with me until four AM weekly because his shift ended at 11PM, and nighttime was his only time to work on graphics. The same guy I paid with cigarettes my mother used to send me that she would get for twenty dollars per carton on an Indian reservation near our house in Rochester, New York. The same guy who face- timed with me overnight from Chicago to Prague, while we stayed up reaching into the ether for design guidance to manifest the Big Murphy's brand logo and branding
graphics.

It was there, inside of that hug, that I felt the spinnaker unravel and fill into the sky as the city lights lit up the night. The view looking north over the Chicago skyline lead me right back to the shores we originally swam on. Back to the first night we met, and stayed up all night working on the entrepreneurial dream in his apartment nearly six years earlier. A twinkle caught our eyes. The white noise of a singing crowd, and a few profound voices carried us into the lounge, then home into our beds to sleep off a night I will always remember.

...

PASSION STITCH

To all of the strangers who have become my dear friends. To the spirit that guided me to them, and to the one that is guiding me still. May we continue to invite into our lives the awareness that from dust we come, and to dust we return. The "in between" is up to us. May it always be ours, not theirs to live. Thank you to all of the gems in my life. The ones that you have now witnessed that emerged from circumstances of chance, good fortune, synchronicity, and massive leaps of faith. Thank you for the priceless role you have all played in the evolution of this knowledge and wisdom brought forth in this text.

Thank you to the people who have powerfully impacted the writing of this book especially but not limited to those you witnessed therein: Hans Phillips, Todd Thompson, Craig Collins, Zachary Bohm, Dr. Greg Reid, Dr. Gene Landrum, Mrs. Marty Padilla, Dr. Daren Martin, Dr. Srini Pillay, Gary Krebs, Alice Hlídkova, Allyn Reid, John Buckingham, Ricardo Pina, Ross Jeffries, Kevin Young, and Dave Kehnast. To my friends at the River North Business Association for making Chicago home, and to all of my loving family members for all of their support from afar.

To my second home at the Metropolitan Club of Chicago on 67. To the view that gave me the inspiration to write these words on many occasions, and to the nights spent there gazing out over the bright lights of the city grid, lighting up a path into in revelation.

And to my dear friends, loved ones, and dream supporters:

Eastern Europe: Čokl, Adam, Petr, Štepan, Tomaš, Barush, Honza, Norbert, Ondra, Franktíška, Kašpar, Luxík, Paní Brožova, Marek, Julča, Žofí, Zuzka, Bara, Jakub, Jiří, Matouš, Tereza, Maruška, Johanna, Daniel, Krak, Michael, Dabout, Marta, Mira, Tommy, Honza, Miš, Oskar, Karol, Marianna, 67, Trafika, Liberal, 22, 16, Namesti Miru, Pavel, Monika, Jitka, Michal, Dalibor, Barney, Ivan, Michal, Monika.
Western Europe: Zé, Bala, João, João, João Baptista, Balzak, David, Alvaro, Pipa Velha, Aduela, Filipa, Rita, Coração, Mercado, Candelabro, Zé, Diogo, Ricardo, Cristina, João, Fred, Tonino.

South America: Ernesto, Hope, Viejo Jack, Adriana, Adriana, Silvia, Carlos, Papacho, Carolina, Adolfo, Julian, Patricia.
Asia: Priyanka, Cia, Raj.

East Coast: Mom, Dad, Ry, Sam, Mike, Phil, Aunt Kath, All Family, Coach Steve, Barber, Mark, Chuck, Rick, Jake, Mandalay, George, Peabs, Sips, Chelsea, HOG, Richard, Lane, Justin, Joe, Ron, Chris, Wes, Bucky, Joe, Deb. Benjamin, Sam, Gary.

Midwest: Alice, Tanya, Matthew, Zach, John, Israel, Victor, Rudy, Juan, Jodit, Royal, Dawit, Royal Souls, Brian, John, Marty, John, Bob, Art, Bob, Zach, Marty, Taylor, Miriam, Deborah, Marissa, Zhenya, Mary, Jim, John, Matt, Betsy, Stacey, Clay, Joonas, Maarit, Adam, Roma, Roman, Melinda, Mikaylo, Eve, Taylor, Mike, Edita, Sarah, Chris, Emily, Miss Meliss, Will, Matt, Mark, Erik, Mr. Parker, Stephen, Charles, Leo, Patrick, Joel, Michael, Christine, Anabel, Matt, Mauro, Kathy V, Luke, Dario, Emily, Danny, and the many others!

West Coast: Greg, Alexis, Kevin, Frank, Brayand, Ray, Allyn, David, Craig, Annie, Raj, Ross, Hans, Dave, Jeff, Craig, Scott, Jason, Kimberly, Stephen.

Southwest: Dr. Daren Martin and Elise Martin.

And, to love: In all of the benevolent ways it has woven itself into my life; romantic, platonic, enigmatic; amorous.

May these words bring light, clarity, and inspiration to all who read them. And may they continue to enrich the hearts, minds, and spirits of all who find them for generations to come.

SOUL STITCH

This book is dedicated to all of the dreamers, thinkers, makers, writers, poets, and entrepreneurs, young and old who choose to acknowledge their intuition as a real muscle, capacity, and layer of existence that although scientifically unproven remains the single most important force we trust to make the moves that count in life.

The time spent writing this book is dedicated to all of the poets and philosophers whose words printed and unprinted I have sifted through over time, and cherished along the way. To the entrepreneurs all around the galaxy striving to explore the final frontier; mind, heart, spirit.

Now good friends, whatever it is you yearn for.

Set the intention, and manifest the steps.

Take them, and keep going.

We are never far.

Always closer.

One

Magic

Moment Away…

Keep stitching, and remember. Get Lost To Find Yourself.

ABOUT THE AUTHOR

Nathan Minnehan has handcrafted over 5000 leather journals. He is an international serial entrepreneur, public speaker, coach, designer, linguist, and founder of walkntalk.com and bigmurphys.com. He is also a custom clothier, making custom suits for well-known leaders around the world.

His suits have been worn by best-selling authors and keynote speakers like Dr. Greg Reid of Three Feet From Gold, Stickability, and Thoughts Are Things; Ross Jeffries of Subtle Words That Sell, King Raj of Authorities, and Frank Shankwitz, creator of the Make-A-Wish Foundation.

Writers around the world in 50 countries and counting use his journals. Business writers like Dr. Daren Martin of Whiteboard, and A Company of Owners also notably use them.

World-class editors like Gary Krebs; former VP and Group Publisher of McGraw Hill and Publisher of Brilliance Audio wear his handmade eyewear.

He has pitched to the original shark from Shark Tank, Kevin Harrington, and helps individuals create transformation in their lives with his custom suits and personal coaching business.

Minnehan began his journey into design as an exchange student in Prague, Czech Republic, and is an avid linguist speaking fluent Czech, Spanish, Portuguese, and English with a goal to speak fifteen languages in the next decade or less.

Minnehan has been featured in:

The Chicago Reader: Dreaming Big In Small Spaces
Study Abroad Magazine: The Road To Success
Time Out Chicago: Steal His Style
POST Rochester: A Natural Born Explorer And His Journals
Huffington Post: Renegade Craft Feature

DESIGN YOUR NEXT CUSTOM SUIT WITH NATHAN!

Nathan with Joel Schaub, after presenting Joel his new blazer with a custom lining.

Nathan and his company Big Murphy's design, produce, and sell:

-Custom Suits, Shirts, Vests, and Overcoats.
-Luxury Leather Bags, Duffles, Briefcases, and Belts.
-Nathan's Team is equipped to make the most quality and luxurious custom garments and leather bags you can dream of!

Contact Nathan's team for a suit or custom garment today!
BigMurphys.com & sales@bigmurphys.com

"5 STARS-After getting a custom suit by Nathan. I have received more compliments and comments than anything I have ever worn."
-Joel Schaub, Chicago's #1 Most well-known Mortgage Lender

BOOK NATHAN AS YOUR NEXT GREAT SPEAKER!

Nathan is available to do:

-Keynotes
-Speaking to Groups and Organizations
-Speaking to Universities and Schools
-Seminars and Training

To contact Nathan's team for inquiries/booking go to:
BookNathan.com

"With the heart of a warrior and spirit of a king, Nathan Minnehan shows you how to be truly great!"

-Dr. Daren Martin, The Culture Architect, A Company Of Owners